The Management Idea Factory

T0384074

> "This book develops a distinctive focus on management consultants as 'knowledge entrepreneurs'. Whereas the bulk of literature has been concerned with the practice and consumption of management ideas, this focus on the ideas generation stage of the consultancy process stresses the crucial role of consultants in the production of management knowledge, as well as filling out our understanding of this important occupational group."
>
> —*Robin Fincham, Stirling Management School, U.K.*

Where do management ideas come from? Although there has traditionally been considerable field-level attention on how management knowledge entrepreneurs market their ideas and practices, there is still a lack of research that discusses the earlier intraorganizational phases in the development process. This is of significance because a lack of knowledge about their 'social life' may hamper the possibility to critical reflect on taken for granted, or at least influential ideas in the world of management.

This book seeks to address this gap by revealing how the development of new ideas and practices takes shape in consultancies. The work addresses questions such as: in which way do consultancies sense the contemporary market needs? How do new ideas and practices become established within a consultancy? How do consultancies seek to maintain their repertoire? And what role do these new ideas and practices play in their assignments? To provide more insight into these different aspects of management idea production, the book draws on and integrates literature from diverse relevant fields such as product innovation and market orientation, but also uses institutional and practice-based perspectives. The research presented in this book can be seen in the light of emerging research into the supply-side dynamics of management ideas that concentrate on empirically studying how knowledge entrepreneurs seek to develop commercially viable ideas and practices that have the potential to have a significant impact on management and organizational praxis.

Stefan Heusinkveld is Associate Professor at the VU University Amsterdam. His research focuses on the production and consumption of management ideas and, in particular, the role of management consultants and management gurus. His work has been published in journals including *Human Relations*, *Journal of Management Studies*, and *Organization Studies*.

 Routledge Studies in Innovation, Organization and Technology

For a full list of titles in this series, please visit www.routledge.com

The Management Idea Factory

Innovation and Commodification in
Management Consulting

Stefan Heusinkveld

Routledge
Taylor & Francis Group

NEW YORK AND LONDON

First published 2014
by Routledge
711 Third Avenue, New York, NY 10017

and by Routledge
2 Park Square, Milton Park, Abingdon, Oxon OX14 4RN

First issued in paperback 2018

*Routledge is an imprint of the Taylor & Francis Group,
an informa business*

Library of Congress Cataloging-in-Publication Data

Heusinkveld, Stefan.
  The management idea factory : innovation and commodification in
management consulting / by Stefan Heusinkveld.
    pages cm. — (Routledge studies in innovation, organization and
technology; 32)
  Includes bibliographical references and index.
  1. Business consultants. 2. Management. I. Title.
  HD69.C6H48   2013
  001—dc23
  2013018677

ISBN 13: 978-1-138-34065-7 (pbk)
ISBN 13: 978-0-415-50330-3 (hbk)

Typeset in Sabon LT
by Apex CoVantage, LLC

Contents

Tables

Acknowledgments

In retrospect, this book can easily be seen as the inevitable result of a research endeavor in seeking to better understand the evolving supply-side dynamics of management ideas. However, like any research journey, the outcome was not as self-evident during the time this project was initiated and performed. Rather, I started this journey with an apparently simple question about how consultants deal with an apparent downswing in the popularity of a management idea. During the process, however, many deviations from the initial inquiry emerged, leading to new fruitful research questions such as: in which way do consultancies sense the contemporary market needs? How do new ideas and practices become established within a consultancy? What role do these new ideas and practices play in their assignments? And: how do experiences in applying ideas feed back into processes of management idea production? Addressing all these relevant questions related to the supply-side dynamics of management ideas urged me to study different theoretical perspectives that allowed developing a fresh view on the data. And it was only when these emerging questions were addressed, I found the basis for returning to the original question with which I initially started this research.

While many of the steps taken were not without substantial difficulties and the outcomes were still highly uncertain, I was fortunate that I did not have to make this research journey on my own. Therefore this book can be seen as truly the product of a collective effort. Indeed, many people helped me in finding my way during this journey which allowed to further specify my initial question, make sense of the data, clarify the choices that I made, position my findings in relation to prior literature, and point me to fruitful directions that I could not have imagined at the start. I am therefore highly indebted to a large number of colleagues with whom I developed the papers that now constitute the basis for this book: Jos Benders, Robert-Jan van den Berg, René ten Bos, Bas Hillebrand, Hajo Reijers, and Klaasjan Visscher.

During my research journey I have also greatly benefited from the helpful comments and suggestions of many scholars who have spent their valuable time on reading preliminary drafts of my papers and providing fruitful answers to many of my questions: Eric Abrahamson, Thomas Armbrüster,

Pojanath Bhatanacharoen, David Brock, Anthony Buono, Lars Engwall, Staffan Furusten, Royston Greenwood, Claudia Groß, Alfred Kieser, Matthias Kipping, Tim Morris, Markus Reihlen, Chris McKenna, Anand Narasimhan, Jurriaan Nijholt, Georges Romme, Kjell-Arne Røvik, David Strang, Andrew Sturdy, Andreas Werr, and Chris Wright. I owe a special thank you to Timothy Clark, Robin Fincham, and Joe O'Mahoney for their brutally honest, but extremely helpful, comments on earlier drafts of the book. Needless to say, I am indebted to many management consultants, whom I cannot mention by name, for their time and a precious glimpse of their experiences within their daily, messy praxis. I would not have been able to draw from such rich data about the conception, development, and application of management ideas without their support. Also my thanks to my 'old' colleagues at the department of Business Administration of the Radboud University in Nijmegen and my 'new' colleagues at the VU University Amsterdam for creating a stimulating and pleasant research environment that provided the necessary support to work on this research.

I am grateful to three different publishers for their permissions to draw on, adapt, and extend material reported earlier in a number of articles that were published elsewhere: (1) *Sage Publications* for Stefan Heusinkveld and Jos Benders, Contested commodification: Consultancies and their struggle with new concept development (*Human Relations*, 2005, 58/3: 283–310), Stefan Heusinkveld and Hajo Reijers, Reflections on a reflective cycle: Building legitimacy in design knowledge development (*Organization Studies*, 2009, 30/8: 865–86), and Stefan Heusinkveld, Jos Benders and Bas Hillebrand, Stretching concepts: The role of competing pressures and decoupling in the evolution of organization concepts (*Organization Studies*, 2013, 34/1: 7–32, (2) *Elsevier* for Stefan Heusinkveld, Jos Benders, and Robert-Jan van den Berg, From market sensing to new concept development in consultancies: The role of information processing and organizational capabilities (*Technovation*, 2009, 29/8: 506–18), and Stefan Heusinkveld and Klaasjan Visscher, Practice what you preach: How consultants frame management concepts as enacted practice (*Scandinavian Journal of Management*, 2012, 28/4: 285–97), (3) *M.E. Sharpe* for Stefan Heusinkveld and Jos Benders, Between professional dedication and corporate design: Exploring forms of new concept development in consultancies (*International Studies of Management and Organization*, 2002, 32/4: 104–22).

Finally, Helma, thank you for your love.

1   Management Ideas as Commodities

Where do management ideas come from? Although ideas such as the BCG-Matrix, 7-S Model, Total Quality Management, Business Process Reengineering, the Balanced Scorecard, Corporate Social Responsibility, Customer Relationship Management, and Lean Management have become widely known among management scholars and management practitioners alike, critical questions about their origin and fabrication are still relatively rare. A management idea, sometimes also referred to as a management concept (Kieser, 1997; Nicolai and Dautwiz, 2010), organization concept (Benders and van Veen, 2001), or management technique (Abrahamson, 1996; David and Strang, 2006; Strang, 2010), is here understood as a more or less coherent prescriptive vision, that includes guidelines for managers and other organizational members regarding how to deal with specific organizational issues, and is known by a particular label (Benders and Verlaar, 2003). Given their inclusion in many standard textbooks on management and organization, some of these ideas have become a taken-for-granted element in the canon of management, or at least seen as an inseparable part of the accepted management vocabulary and related processes of socialization (ten Bos, 2000; Sahlin-Andersson and Engwall, 2002). For students of management, and organizations that employ managers, business school curricula have become 'unthinkable' without some explicit attention to these ideas, or their successors.

Unsurprisingly, given that an increasing number of today's managers have received some form of formal management education, management ideas are often considered central to managers' occupational identities and constitutive for their sense of self (Jackson, 2001; Clark and Salaman, 1998; Sturdy et al., 2006; ten Bos, 2000; Parker, 2002). This will increase the likelihood that they will draw upon these ideas in framing complex organizational processes (Cornelissen, 2011), to legitimate decisions that they make (Astley and Zammuto, 1992), to acquire social status in the management community (Huczynski, 1993), and constitute an important precondition in adequate communications with other management practitioners such as colleagues and consultants (Clark and Salaman, 1998; Wilhelm and Bort, 2013). Given the assumed defining role of these ideas in the world of management, scholarly and managerial discourses remain remarkably silent about the social practices that have produced them beyond some general assumptions and insightful anecdotal evidence (e.g. Crainer, 1997; O'Shea and Madigan, 1997). This is a nontrivial issue given that concealing the way these ideas are fabricated may tarnish a critical assessment of their broader values, the underlying interests and beliefs of those who produced them, limit the recognition of viable alternatives, and impede an adequate understanding of their impact on management and organizational practice.

MANAGEMENT KNOWLEDGE COMMODIFICATION

In seeking to shed more light on the intricate puzzles related to the central question I started this book with, various theorists have stressed that these management ideas do not emerge fully developed out of nothing (Peterson, 1979; Abrahamson, 1996), are not the product of a sole genius (Becker, 1974; Clark, 2004; Clark and Greatbatch, 2004), neither can these ideas be understood as universally detached from any cultural and historical roots (Guillén, 1994; Grint 1994; Shenhav, 1999), nor are they an unavoidable exponent of progress in management research (Jacques, 1996; Lammers, 1988). Rather, an influential stream of research posits that these management ideas should be seen as the result of processes of productivization (Huczynski, 1993) or commodification (Fincham, 1995) which, according to Suddaby and Greenwood involves: 'the conversion of localized, experiential and highly contingent managerial knowledge into a reified, commercially valuable form presented as objective, ahistorical and having universal principles' (2001: 938). Here particular research attention has been given to the role of various knowledge entrepreneurs such as management consultants, management gurus, business schools, and seminar organizers involved in transforming management knowledge into a packaged and commercially valuable form that can be bought and sold on a market for management solutions (Fincham, 1995; Abrahamson, 1996; Carter and Crowther, 2000; Sturdy and Gabriel, 2000). Management scholars even consider knowledge commodification as a key element in understanding the growing supply of management solutions and the expansion of the management knowledge industry (Sahlin-Andersson and Engwall, 2002). Following Suddaby and Greenwood (2001), using the notion of commodification has been important because it has provided a number of useful insights which allowed gaining better insight into the emergence, prevalence, and perceived value of particular management ideas.

First, drawing on a commodification perspective allows better understanding of the skepticism and criticism that many popular management ideas or 'fads' attracted and how this relates to important concerns of treating management knowledge as a property that can be bought and sold on a market for solutions. Ten Bos and Heusinkveld (2007) distinguished between rationalist and humanistic-political approaches. They suggest that rationalist criticism sees the apparent mass production of commodified forms of management knowledge as an unwarranted simplification of the real complexities of organizations (McGill, 1988), and the knowledge commodities even as dangerous, amoral, or 'sick', potentially undermining the foundations of organizations' competitive advantage (e.g. Hilmer and Donaldson, 1996; Micklethwait and Wooldridge, 1996; Sorge and van Witteloostuijn, 2004). Certainly, the process has been regarded as being significantly at odds with the academic ideal of knowledge development and accumulation (Kieser, 2002; Lammers, 1988; Guillén, 1994). Humanistic-political approaches have focused more on the negative consequences for employees of the new knowledge commodities and their application in organizations such as 'more stressful' working conditions and a tendency to privilege the interests of certain groups within and outside the organization over those of employees or other stakeholders (Grint, 1994; Grint and Case, 1998; Knights and McCabe, 1998).

Second, by focusing on an object's exchange value in a market economy rather than only its (technical) use value, the notion of commodification contributes to understanding that management ideas have many different functions for knowledge entrepreneurs (Werr et al., 1997; Morris, 2001), not the least to enhance the possibility to be 'exchanged' and thereby generate business (Carter and Crowther, 2000; Fincham, 1995). Kieser assumes such packaged forms of knowledge better allows attracting clients '. . . as these create the impression that the methods of the respective management concept have been tested in many companies' (2002: 168). As a result, important research attention has been given to the central attributes of commercially successful management ideas. Indeed, a substantial body of literature focuses on a number of key elements contained in the rhetoric of these ideas such as promises of significant performance improvement, references to successful consumers, easily understandable figures and vocabularies, and conceptual ambiguity (Benders and van Veen, 2001; Kieser, 1997). These elements are assumed to enhance an idea's exchange value, thereby increasing the likelihood to become saleable and ultimately viable moneymaking items.

Third, another important insight offered by a commodification perspective lies in recognizing that the objectivation of management knowledge products may alienate potential 'consumers' from the social practices that have produced these ideas. As Suddaby and Greenwood phrase: 'Services produced for exchange, thus, become detached from their producers and become objectified' (2001: 944). For instance, Berglund and Werr (2000) stressed that consultants aim to present their knowledge products as objectified and universal, while at the same time propagate the necessity of drawing on consulting expertise to recontextualize the abstracted principles. Therefore, in line with Becker's (1974) and Peterson's (1979) renowned work on the production of cultural artifacts, theorists emphasized the significance of not treating successful knowledge commodities as given, but to focus on a series of crucial activities designed to transform management knowledge into a codified and abstracted from (Abrahamson, 1996; Suddaby and Greenwood, 2001). Moreover studies have shown how management knowledge can be considered as 'collective social product' (Clark and Greatbatch, 2004: 410) that is shaped in the interaction between different relevant constituencies. Thus rather than being concerned with contents or accepting a reified account of a knowledge commodity's history (Shenhav, 1999) that is constructed to gain legitimacy, a commodification perspective focuses on 'issues about how and why certain types of knowledge are produced' (Suddaby and Greenwood, 2001: 944).

Finally, the notion of commodification has contributed to explaining the continued supply and replacement of one management idea by another. In his seminal work, Huczynski frames this phenomenon in terms of 'planned obsolescence', which, in his words entails that: 'A producer can enter the management idea market with the confidence that a particular product which is selling well will be displaced at a future time' (1993: 285). In line with this, theorists have stressed that knowledge entrepreneurs continuously have to invest in the development and commercialization of new commodities to keep their portfolio in tune with market demand (Gill and Whittle, 1993; Clark and Greatbatch, 2004). Indeed, maintaining a knowledge commodity that has fallen out of fashion is likely detrimental to a knowledge entrepreneurs' legitimacy in the market (Kipping, 1999; McKenna, 2006). For instance, McKinsey's reputation on the Multidivisional model in the 1960s led to serious problems for this consulting firm when many large business organizations no longer considered this model as state-of-the art or useful. The attention for this commodity witnessed a significant decline and demand for 'Multidivisionalization' dropped off by the early 1970s. As a result, at the McKinsey offices: 'somewhere about the 1970 the phone stopped ringing' (McKenna, 1997: 230). Applying the notion of commodification thus focuses attention to an increased competition and a 'spiraling need for new ideas and practices' (Suddaby and Greenwood, 2001: 945) that is induced by the fact that commodified forms of management knowledge can be more easily commensurated and imitated (O'Mahoney, Heusinkveld and Wright, 2013).

THE 'SOCIAL LIFE' OF COMMODITIES

As discussed above, prior literature on management knowledge commodification has significantly furthered our insight into the supply-side dynamics of management ideas in various ways, yet little is known about a commodity's 'social life' (Appadurai, 2005) or 'cultural biography' (Kopytoff, 1986), an essential element in developing a more comprehensive understanding of commodification (Ertman and Williams, 2005). The concept of commodity has a long history in social and (political) economic theory (see also O'Mahoney et al., 2013). Marx's treatise of commodity fetishism in the first parts of his seminal work *Capital* is considered one of the earliest and unquestionably the most influential, albeit controversial, understanding of commodity and commodification (Appadurai, 1986; Bocock, 1993; Corrigan, 1997; Ertman and Williams, 2005; Fine, 2002). In contrast to feudal or preindustrial modes of production in which goods are typically manufactured for direct use, Marx explained that under industrial capitalism, goods are primarily produced for market exchange (Bocock, 1993). He sees commodity fetishism as unavoidably intertwined with privileging goods' exchange value over their use value. This entails that through the mechanisms of market exchange, not only goods are reified into an object representing a particular exchange value, but also the 'underlying' labor is put in economic terms and 'brought into equivalence with one another' (Fine, 2002: 35), while the social activity that produced these commodities remain hidden in the marketplace resulting in 'alienation of workers from the products of their labor' (Bocock, 1993: 36).

While various theorists have fruitfully developed the notion of commodity and commodity fetishism further, it has also been widely drawn upon in different fields of research such as law, sociology, anthropology, religious studies, literary studies, philosophy, and management to examine and critically asses contemporary phenomena that have occurred in these fields. A fundamental issue in these writings involves whether and how people and objects should be interpreted in economic terms and subjected to market principles, or to put it succinctly 'what should be the scope of marketization?' (Ertman and Williams, 2005: 2). For instance, the notion of commodification is often used to critically discuss the conceptualization and treatise of a large variety of different subjects and objects such as slaves (Kopytoff, 1982), religious items (Sinha, 2011), sex, children, and body parts (Radin, 2001), policing and security (Loader, 1999), information (Adair, 2010), knowledge (Hellström and Raman, 2001; Lyotard, 1984), academic research (Radder, 2010), academic labor (Willmott, 1995), management knowledge (Fincham, 1995), (mass) culture (DuGay, 1996; Gilbert, 2008), and teaching (Sturdy and Gabriel, 2000) as commodities. Obviously, this list is far from complete, but it may give a brief impression of the breadth of different phenomena that are analyzed in this light and perhaps is indicative for the widespread appeal of Marx' framework, and the value that is attributed to pointing to the dangers of commodity fetishism and the underlying capitalist ideology that prevails in contemporary societies.

In any case, it is important to recognize that these analyses typically provide a critical view of the possibilities and limitations of putting 'things' in terms of exchange value. A characteristic example comes from Willmott (1995) who explains the institutional and political conditions under which academic labor is framed in terms of quasi exchange value. He argues that: 'Individual academics, departments and institutions are currently being offered incentives to derive a sense of purpose and identity less from the substantive relationships with students, or even from their capacity to foster a supportive environment for scholarship and research, and more from the rankings they achieve' (Willmott, 1995: 1024). In a similar way Radder (2010) has developed a philosophical critique on the practices of commodified academic research that, in his view, have a number of important undesirable or even harmful consequences such as less robust research methods, higher levels of secrecies, narrow focus on short-term achievements, and privatization of public knowledge.

An emerging line of work stressed the importance of moving beyond solely understanding commodities and commodification in relation to classic skepticism of marketization and underlying logics of capitalism. Here prior literature on commodification is criticized for being too much concerned with emphasizing and elucidating the limitations of interpreting 'things' in economic terms. Williams and Zelizer even state that the central question that dominates much of the literature, that is, 'to commodify or not to commodify?' (2005: 363), while useful and informative in itself, constitutes a restricted question that may impede further productive inquiries and limit the development of complementary fruitful understandings. Drawing on a cultural perspective, and in particular anthropological work on the biography approach, Kopytoff (1986) has developed a more processual conceptualization of commodification that allows for the possibility that 'things' have their own 'lives' which comprises cultural and cognitive processes that continuously redefines the social status of a 'thing' other than only in commodity terms (see also Appadurai, 1986; Corrigan, 1997). To illustrate how commodities may be better seen as a specific stage in the life of 'things', Kopytoff rather provocatively draws from the example of slavery (see also Kopytoff, 1982). He suggests that slavery, albeit morally reprehensible, cannot be seen as a stable and homogeneous status, but as a process in which the slave is continuously redefined as he or she may move into and out of the sphere of exchange. Thus, this assumes that the social status of commodities is fundamentally indeterminate, or in the words of Kopytoff: '. . . when the commodity is effectively out of the commodity sphere, its status is inevitably ambiguous and open to the push and pull of events and desires, as it is shuffled about in the flux of life' (1986: 83). Building on this conceptualization, Appadurai (1986; 2005) stressed that to better understand the 'commodity condition', that is, when the exchangeability is considered a socially relevant status somewhere in the life of a 'thing', research should focus on the intersection between (1) the stage in a commodity's cultural biography, (2) the degree of marketability or more broadly the measures by which potential commodities are perceived, and (3) the specific social arena(s) within which a (potential) commodity resides.

Our discussion about commodities and commodification, albeit by no means complete in itself, aims to set an agenda for more systematic research on our central question about the supply-side dynamics of management ideas. Drawing from the literature on commodification we indicate that it preludes prior discussions on management knowledge commodification and allows shedding more light on its social life or cultural biography, an issue that received scant attention in the literature about the production of management ideas and the management knowledge industry beyond the assumption that management knowledge commodities or their marketability follow a life cycle (Abrahamson and Fairchild, 1999; Gill and Whittle, 1993; Suddaby and Greenwood, 2001).

Thus in the context of management ideas, these debates about commodification may alert us that gaining further insight into the 'commodity situation' of management idea goes beyond focusing only on the moment or state of an idea's exchange, or as Appadurai plead, such a view allows: 'breaking significantly with the production-dominated Marxian view of the commodity and focusing on its total trajectory from production through change/ distribution, to consumption' (2005: 36). Similarly, the influential work of Czarniawska and Sevón (1996) refer to the translation of management ideas as an ongoing, dynamic process prior to and after a commodity is launched on the market for managerial solutions. However, prior analyses of management knowledge commodities are primarily based on a limited number of key characteristics or phases in isolation and treat these commodities as stable products, primarily modified during their implementation to 'fit' local contexts (Ansari et al., 2010; Nicolai and Dautwiz, 2010; Strang, 2010). Thus although insightful at a generic level, prior literature has paid scant attention to the important complexities that stem from a knowledge commodity's social life outside of the exchange sphere. Therefore it is important to develop an adequate understanding of the variety of 'social arenas' (Appadurai, 2005: 37) in which a potential commodity resides during the different stages in its life.

PURPOSE OF THE BOOK

This book aims to contribute to debates about the supply-side dynamics of management ideas by exploring the way management consultants construct management ideas throughout different stages in its social life. I particularly focus on the way these consultants are involved in what is dubbed as new concept development (Heusinkveld and Benders, 2005), or knowledge-based innovation (Anand et al., 2007). It contributes to showing the significance of considering and studying the everyday processes of idea production thereby gaining further insight into a commodity's social life, or in the words of Peterson and Anand: 'culture being shaped in the mundane processes of their production' (2004: 312). These processes remain often invisible or become reified (Shenhav, 1999) because of processes that induce collective forgetfulness (Lammers, 1988; Brunsson and Olsen, 1997), narrow-minded managerialist and utopian orientations (Parker, 2002; ten Bos, 2000), or as part of systematic efforts to create a favorable image thereby enhancing a commodity's exchange value (Carter and Crowther, 2000; Kieser, 1997). Editing out a commodity's social life from the canon of management will likely disconnect students of management from the social practices and related interests, intentions, and belief systems that shape the way potentially influential management ideas are fabricated.

The research presented in this book can therefore be seen in the light of emerging research into the supply-side dynamic (Clark and Greatbatch, 2004) that concentrate on empirically studying how knowledge entrepreneurs seek to develop commercially viable ideas that have the potential to have a significant impact on management and organizational praxis. The work addresses questions that are relevant in understanding biography of commodified forms of management knowledge: in which way do consultancies sense the contemporary market needs? How do new ideas and practices become established within a consultancy? What role do these new ideas and practices play in their assignments and how does this feed back into processes of management idea production? And how do consultancies seek to maintain their repertoire in a stage of decline?

To provide more insight into these different aspects of innovation and commodification in consultancies, the book draws on and synthesizes literature from diverse relevant fields of research such as market orientation (Day, 1994), product innovation (e.g. Dougherty and Heller, 1994), but also applies practice-based (e.g. Jarzabkowski, 2004) and institutional perspectives (e.g. Oliver, 1991) which are used as theoretical backdrops in analyzing the different stages in a commodity's social life. Using print media data, interview data of a large number of consultants from different consultancies, and two in-depth case studies within two consultancies as an empirical basis, the present work seeks to trace new ideas and practices back to their fabrication. Focusing on an idea's social life, that is, the way relevant social actors interpret and how an idea moves from a given point of departure through various phases to some kind of end state (see also van de Ven, 1992) allows for a better understanding of the sociopolitical process in which new management ideas–especially those that may have a significant impact on the managerial masses–gain 'good currency' and evolve within consultancies. The central point of this research is to reveal how widely accepted ideas are not necessarily so self-evident during the time they are constructed and add support to the notion that the development of new management ideas is neither a homogeneous nor straightforward matter. As a result, the book can at the same time be read as (1) an account of the way innovation and commodification takes shape in management consultancies, (2) an analysis of the development and evolution of management ideas, and the production of cultural artifacts more generally, and (3) a demystification of or at least a critical reflection on taken–for–granted and influential ideas in the world of management.

The central research question 'where do management ideas come from?' is part of a larger puzzle about the creation, dissemination, and impact of management ideas on management and organizational practice (Sturdy, 2004), but also about intricate questions on dealing with important complexities and ambiguities inherent to studying ideational phenomena and the related creative production processes congruent to aesthetic fashion, art works, films, and music (Hirsch, 1972; Becker, 1974; Peterson, 1979). Issues around the social life and consequences of ideas comprise challenging issues for several reasons, not the least because management ideas are widely recognized as especially ambiguous or lacking in clear material outcomes (Alvesson, 1993; Benders and Van Veen, 2001; Nijholt and Benders, 2010). A related complication in studying the social life of ideas lies in the likelihood of retrospective reconstruction of events and experiences (Miller et al., 1997) by selectively tracing the trajectories of the 'winners' (Shenhav, 1999).

Finally, relating the notion of 'innovation', 'novelty', or 'new' to management consultancies' products and services has always been a contested endeavor (Taminiau et al., 2009). Indeed, while some may consider consultancies as 'innovation factories' (Hargadon and Sutton, 2000: 161, cited in O'Mahoney, 2010) and producing state of the art knowledge (Sarvary, 1999), others may more or less forcefully challenge such a claim by showing how the products and services that are presented as 'new' do not differ much from 'old' insights (Kieser, 1996; Lammers, 1988) or clients' existing knowledge (Sturdy et al., 2006). Brunsson and Olsen even stress that consultants are '. . . in a particularly good position for initiating and pursuing the same reform in new organizations [. . .]. Forgetfulness is their key competence' (1997: 42). In addition, various studies have shown that innovation in the context of consulting not only originates from a large variety of knowledge sources, but also relate to different knowledge items such as 'new' service delivery processes, tools, presentations, training programs, white papers, books, and articles (de Caluwé and de Man, 2010; O'Mahoney, 2011). Whatever the case, to shed more light on the production of management ideas, this book takes an open-ended view by focusing on the ideas and underlying repertoires that are 'perceived as new' (Rogers, 1995: 11) by consultants. This requires drawing on a verstehende attitude (Wester, 1995), which entails in this research trying to understand how people who are widely involved in the 'handling' of commodified forms of management knowledge construct the 'lives' of management ideas they produce from initial conception to maturity and decline and how they attach meaning to the development of a broader repertoire that will contribute to the commercialization and implementation of these ideas (Werr et al., 1997; Werr and Stjernberg, 2003; Heusinkveld and Benders, 2005).

Before further detailing the conceptual background and research method in chapter 2, I provide a brief description of management consultancies as theoretically relevant research context and their relation to management knowledge commodities.

RESEARCH CONTEXT: MANAGEMENT CONSULTING FIRMS

A deeper study of the way consultants are involved in what is dubbed new concept development or knowledge-based innovation offers a relevant research context to further explore the different stages in the cultural biography of commodified forms of management knowledge for at least two key reasons.

First, consultants are widely regarded as important producers and propagators of commodified forms of management knowledge on the market for managerial solutions (Abrahamson, 1996; Kieser, 1997; Suddaby and Greenwood, 2001; Faust, 2002; Anand et al., 2007; O'Mahoney, 2010). Suddaby and Greenwood even argue that the commodification of management knowledge: 'takes place primarily within management consulting firms' (2001: 942; see also Kieser, 2002). Indeed, historical accounts indicate that management knowledge commodities have always played a fundamental role in the way consultancies have legitimized their existence, created their business, and intervened in organizations (Guillén, 1994; Kipping, 1999; Wright, 2002; McKenna, 2006). For instance, various scientific management techniques and the Bedaux system of work measurement are regarded as important determinants in the expansion of pioneering management consultancies in the 1920s and 1930s (Kipping, 2002). During the 1960s, a firm like McKinsey extensively encouraged the dissemination of the multidivisional model across European countries (McKenna, 2006). A few years later, consultants from the Boston Consulting Group became widely renowned for their portfolio matrix. More recently, David and Strang (2006) demonstrated how consultancies went into the market for Total Quality Management (TQM) when this idea was becoming fashionable in the early 1980s.

Not surprisingly, therefore, repeatedly introducing 'new' commodities may act as important vehicle for generating business and may contribute to a reputation as an innovative knowledge provider (Fincham and Evans, 1999; Kieser, 2002; Wright and Kitay, 2004). For instance, CSC Index, as one of the initial propagators of Business Process Re-engineering (BPR), was able to expand their revenues from $30 million in 1988 to $150 million in 1993 (Jackson, 1996: 576). Similarly, Gemini Consulting generated considerable revenues from the sales of their 'Business Transformation' concept (O'Shea and Madigan, 1997), and McKinsey not only significantly increased its profits in the 1960s by 'supplying' the multidivisional model (Kipping, 1999), it was also able to re-emerge as 'the preeminent management consulting firm' through its popularization of its 7S-model and 'corporate culture' concepts in the 1980s (McKenna, 2006: 214). At the same time, critical accounts have stressed that consultants take advantage of clients by talking problems into organizations playing upon managers' anxiety in order to sell their predefined commodities (O'Shea and Madigan, 1997; Pinault, 2000; Kieser, 2002; Craig, 2005). For instance, O'Shea and Madigan (1997: 189) emphasize that the consulting industry is renowned for its 'propensity for presenting fads as solution to problems'. Kieser (2002: 180) even argues that: 'consultants who compile a new management concept also construct the business problem for which the offered solution fits'.

Second, consultants are not only considered important management knowledge commodifiers and propagators of these commodities on 'public display' (Furusten, 1999; Faust, 2002; Braam et al., 2007), but are also often deeply involved in actual change projects that are induced or associated with these commodities (Bloomfield and Danieli, 1995; O'Shea and Madigan, 1997; Sturdy et al., 2009; O'Mahoney, 2010). For instance, the study of Wright and Kitay (2004) shows how apart from consultants' involvement in the large-scale proliferation of the Employee Relations model on a market level, they also heavily drew on this management idea in their day-to-day work with clients, that is, at the level of a consulting project (see also Benders et al., 1998; Whittle, 2005). However, there is debate on the nature of these ideas' impact on management and organizational practice. Functionalist approaches place more emphasis on the likelihood of enhanced performance levels of client organizations exemplified by different 'success stories', narrating a number of key points that have been crucial in the successful implementation of a management idea (e.g. Greiner and Metzger, 1983). More critical views suggest that these narratives represent a selective image of the way organizations deploy a new idea, since difficulties in implementation or contentious issues tend to be glossed over (Kieser, 1997; Furusten, 1999; Røvik, 2002). Sturdy explained that important difficulties in establishing the potential impact of management consultants relate to notable methodological issues in prior research and the 'diffuse and changing boundaries between consultancy and management' (2011: 521).

Another stream of critical accounts that provide support for the important role of consultants in the application of 'new' forms of commodified knowledge often emphasizes the substantial negative consequences for employees (O'Shea and Madigan, 1997; Knights and McCabe, 1998; Craig, 2005). For example, O'Shea and Madigan (1997) draw on cases of the implementation of the Transformation concept by Gemini Consulting. They show how the consultants' application of their commodity had substantial consequences for the client organization: 'these efforts involved sweeping change and left their share of victims in their wakes, the displaced middle managers at Cigna, the nurses and staff and middle managers at Montgomery General who saw their jobs disappear' (1997: 198). At the same time these authors show that the consultancy generated not only substantial revenues from these projects, but also valuable experiences which they could sell to other clients in the same sector: 'The smart companies walk away not only with fat checks, but with something that is much more valuable over the long run, experience in a particular industry' (1997: 204).

While there remains debate about the sources of management knowledge commodities, the way they are propagated, how they are applied, and their possible consequences for organizations as well as for employees, management consultancies can be considered a theoretically relevant and fruitful research context to shed further light on the supply-side dynamics of management ideas. Obviously, by focusing this research on how consultants construct an idea's social life I highlight only one side of the coin (cf. O'Mahoney et al., 2013), but given the consultants' assumed widespread involvement in the dissemination of commodities and their application in organizations, I believe this constitutes a necessary and important step in shedding more light on the social processes of management knowledge commodification, to develop a more enhanced conceptualization of the possible impact of knowledge entrepreneurs and their ideas on management and organizational practice.

OUTLINE OF THE BOOK

After the two introductory chapters, this book comprises five further chapters, each focusing on one key stage in the social life of management knowledge commodities. In chapter 2 I first outline extant understandings of the commodification of management knowledge in the prior literature. Specifically, I elaborate on central approaches in understanding commodified forms of management knowledge and outline a number of commonalities and differences. In the final section of this second chapter I explain the empirical approach that is followed in the research reported in this book.

Chapter 3 concentrates on the aspect of market sensing. Although theorists often emphasize the importance of the interaction between 'commodifier' and consumer, the issue of market sensing has received scant attention in current discussions on management knowledge commodification and management consultancies. To address this issue, this chapter explores the process by which management consultants acquire, interpret, and utilize client information in the context of the development of new management ideas. Drawing on the market orientation literature, this chapter provides an understanding of how customer needs play a role in commodification processes and how this is considered to be crucial to the success of a new management idea.

Chapter 4 seeks to develop a deeper understanding of the specific way that key activities in relation to management knowledge commodification take shape in consultancies. Using the innovation literature as a starting point, the chapter reveals that the way these activities are carried out varies considerably among different firms and each form shows substantial inadequacies. As a result, this research reflects the need to place greater emphasis on the different forms of commodification activities and trajectories in consultancies and how these firms deal with the significant tensions associated with each form.

In chapter 5, the book turns to the internal legitimation and establishment of new management ideas. Although theorists have stressed that relevant activities occur long before a new idea is introduced on the market, the process of knowledge commodification is often presented as linear and unproblematic, as merely being concerned with jointly turning new ideas into marketable services. Drawing on a product innovation perspective, the chapter discusses several major impediments to linking development efforts to the consultancy, and indicates the importance of considering the process in which management ideas gain 'good currency'.

Chapter 6 elucidates how management consultants construct management ideas as enacted practice in the context of a client-consultant relationship. Despite the recognition that management consultants are also widely involved in their application within organizations, little academic attention has been devoted to the way they understand the deployment of commodified forms of management knowledge in relation to their assignments. Drawing on a practice-based perspective, this chapter discusses key framing moves that are used by consultants to make sense of and justify the deployment of management ideas and explain how these may restrict or enlarge the perceived determining role of commodified forms of management knowledge within a client organization.

The seventh chapter focuses on how consultants respond when a management idea tends to go out of vogue. Despite the recognition of management consultants as important fashion setters, little is known about the actual strategies management consultants use to deal with a downswing in the popularity of commodified forms of management knowledge. Drawing on the notion of 'decoupling', this chapter identifies distinct response strategies and shows how these are systematically associated with multiple pressures and comprise different implications for the form of a commodity.

In the concluding chapter the results of the preceding chapters are synthesized and reconsidered for carving out the implications for better understanding the supply-side dynamics of management ideas. It is argued that, to further insight into the key question: where do management ideas come from, there is a need to look beyond the 'commodity situation' and study their cultural biography, that is, the way relevant social actors construct commodified forms of management knowledge throughout different stages of their social life. This allows showing how widely known and taken-for-granted ideas in the world of management can be seen as the result of different collective social processes of productivization or commodification (see also Becker, 1974; Peterson, 1979) that comprise different routes, are propelled by various and sometimes competing key drivers and occur in distinct social environments, and ultimately allow defining unexplored areas fruitful to new research.

2 Studying Management Idea Production

The first chapter has shown that the concept of commodification can be fruitfully applied to address the central research question because it preludes prior discussions on the supply-side dynamics of management ideas and allows shedding more light on its 'social live' or 'cultural biography', an issue that received scant attention in the literature about the production of management ideas and the management knowledge industry. In this chapter I review prior literature on management research on knowledge commodification thereby particularly focusing on three central areas of research as well as identifying and specifying the key findings and debates within these distinct areas. This is followed by an explanation of the research method that has been followed in this work. In chapters 3–7 I present the results of the empirical analyses by elaborating on a variety of relevant themes in the 'social life' of a management idea. The final section discusses the theoretical implications of our analysis for extant understandings of the production of management ideas and provides a number of fruitful directions for future research.

In the field of management research, knowledge commodification is generally considered an important element in understanding the widespread popularity of knowledge entrepreneurs and their standardized management solutions (Abrahamson, 1996; Suddaby and Greenwood, 2001; Sahlin-Andersson and Engwall, 2002; David and Strang, 2006). Here commodification is often referred to as the process of transforming management knowledge into a particular form that can be sold on a market for management solutions. It is argued that that, on this market, various knowledge entrepreneurs are involved in 'productivizing' management knowledge into a packaged and commercially valuable commodity (Huczynski, 1993). This is often understood as driven by the interests of many actors in enhancing the exchange value of management knowledge. As outlined in chapter 1, opinions about management knowledge commodification differ substantially in the prior literature. Some theorists use a commodification perspective to draw out a number of important advantages such as facilitating the marketing of one's expertise, better addressing the clients' needs, improving the ability to colonize new territories, and increasing leveraging capacity (O'Mahoney et al., 2013). Other, more critical accounts, understand commodification as being significantly at odds with the academic ideal of knowledge development and accumulation (Kieser, 2002; Lammers, 1988) and point to the potentially negative consequences for employees such as 'more stressful' working conditions when deploying these ideas in organizations (Grint and Case, 1998; Knights and McCabe, 1998).

In the next sections I focus on what ten Bos and Heusinkveld (2007) labeled as the 'explanatory approach'. This latter strand of research does not seek to promote or condemn commodification as such, but focuses on explaining how and why certain commodified forms of management knowledge have become so attractive among the managerial masses. In particular I discuss three major strands of research that can be distinguished in the literature on management knowledge commodification. It will be argued that the prior literature has provided important insights into (1) the form in which these commodities are marketed, (2) the specific characteristics of the commodification process, and (3) the way commodities evolve over time (see Table 2.1).

Table 2.1 Perspectives on management knowledge commodification

	Form	Process	Evolution
Key question	In what form are management ideas presented on the management knowledge market?	How are management ideas created and processed prior to their launch on the management knowledge market?	How do management ideas evolve once introduced on the management knowledge market?
Focus of analysis	Key characteristics of management ideas that enhance their market value.	Vital activities (and their sequence) necessary for transforming management knowledge into a form that can be sold.	Main lifecycle-trajectories of commercially valuable management ideas and their antecedents.
Representative examples	Fincham (1995); Kieser (1997); ten Bos (2000); Benders and van Veen (2001); Jackson (2001); Røvik (2002); Clark and Greatbatch (2004)	Huczynki (1993); Abrahamson (1996); Suddaby and Greenwood (2001); Birkinshaw (2010); Reihlen and Nikolova (2010)	Lammers (1988); Barley and Kunda (1992); Gill and Whittle (1993); Jacques (1996); Abrahamson and Fairchild (1999); Nijholt and Benders (2007)

Form of Knowledge Commodities

Theorists have given much attention to the form in which these management knowledge commodities are presented on the market for management solutions (Huczynski, 1993; Fincham, 1995; Kieser, 1997; Furusten, 1999; ten Bos, 2000). One important stream of research focuses mainly on analyzing the key characteristics of successful management knowledge commodities (see Table 2.2). These accounts have provided crucial insights into the necessary (but individually not sufficient) conditions for knowledge commodities so as to be inherently attractive and accessible to managers (Strang and Meyer, 1993). In line with the seminal work of Davis (1986) who attributed the broad appeal of particular classic social theories not only to their contents but also to what he dubbed as their 'rhetorical programme that spoke to their audience's common concerns' (1986: 298), various theorists have stressed the importance of studying how some key rhetorical features or 'textual conventions' (Clark and Greatbatch, 2004: 411) that are expected to increase a commodity's market value and enhance the possibility to become widely received among the managerial masses (Fincham, 1995; Suddaby and Greenwood, 2001).

Building on the work of the philosopher Hans Achterhuis, ten Bos (2000) even argued that many popular management ideas are infused with utopian tendencies that make them inherently more attractive than the

Table 2.2   Characteristics of successful management ideas

Key characteristic	Representative work
Simplification/easily readable	Huczynski (1993); Fincham (1995); Kieser (1997); Clark and Greatbatch (2004)
Substantial performance improvement	Abrahamson (1996); ten Bos (2000)
Universalization	Suddaby and Greenwood (2001); Rvik (2002)
Social authorization	Jackson (1996); Furusten (1999); Rvik (2002); Clark and Greatbatch (2004)
Interpretative viability/vagueness	Kieser (1997); Benders and van Veen (2001); Giroux (2006)
Supporting manager identity	Jackson (1996); Clark and Salaman (1998); Wilhelm and Bort (2013)
Fit with zeitgeist	Barley and Kunda (1992); Grint (1994); Abrahamson and Fairchild (1999); Shenhav (1999); Abrahamson and Eisenmann (2008)

difficulties and problems inherent to existing managerial ideas and practices. Indeed, ten Bos' outstanding and comprehensive analysis shows that
central management ideas in the broad areas of strategy, leadership, culture,
learning, and organizational design contain important rational-utopian elements such as betterment of the collective, malleability of dreams, good-
ness of human beings, radicalism, functionality, obsession with hygiene,
productivity, and happiness in an utilitarian sense (2000: 12–13). Abrahamson (1996) argued that an essential function of such rhetoric is to create
a belief among management practitioners that a particular commodity is
the most efficient and progressive means to address an 'essential' performance gap. For instance, the 'problem discourse' about Quality Circles
emphasized the danger of global competition and related the economic
success of other countries to their specific work practices, while 'solution discourse' theorizes this commodity as a successful, all-powerful, and
problem-free answer that could counter the relevant threats (Abrahamson
and Fairchild, 1999; Cole, 1999). Similarly, various theorists have shown
that there are different ways in which rhetorical forms used to attain this
function (Strang and Meyer, 1993; Barley and Kunda, 1992; Abrahamson
and Eisenmann, 2008).

For instance, by analyzing six popular families of management ideas,
Huczynski (1993) identified in his seminal work three main recurring, related, and overlapping themes in these ideas. While these themes are hypothesized to contribute to a commodity's popularity, Huczynski stressed
that: 'factors other than just content of the management idea itself play a
part in securing popular status for it' (1993: 113). A first set of characteristics relates to an idea's direct usefulness to managers in helping to understanding their daily work and comprise elements such as putting intricate
managerial issues in relatively uncomplicated terminology, focusing on individual behavior and emphasizing the malleability of organizational members. Second, another broad theme that can be found in popular ideas refers
to what Huczynski phrases as: 'managers' need to maintain and enhance
their own self-esteem and gain the esteem of others' (1993: 74). This relates
to elements such as legitimating the role and leadership of management in
contemporary organizations, the shared interest of organizational members,
and the possibility of adapting the knowledge commodity by users. A third
and final theme involves a focus on how abstract principles can be translated into concrete guidelines and practical action. Huczynski (1993) argued
that this focus on practical application is accomplished by various elements
in the ideas such as guiding principles, claims of universal applicability and
credibility, as well as an indication that the idea will have positive results on
the short term.

Also the influential research of Kieser (1997) indicates the importance of
various rhetorical techniques used by knowledge entrepreneurs. Drawing on
theories of fashions in aesthetic forms his analysis identifies 10 key rhetorical

elements that can be found in best-selling books. Unlike Abrahamson's (1996) account, Kieser does not only focus on the rhetorical elements which directly contribute to the perceived value of a commodity, such as emphasizing the obsolescence of old ideas, relating a commodity to widely accepted values, and linking it to scientific research. Rather Kieser's work also emphasizes the importance of the way this perceived value is communicated. Indeed, a key element to become widely appreciated by knowledge consumers relates to presenting ideas in an accessible form (Clark and Greatbatch, 2004; Kieser, 1997). This entails that to enhance a knowledge commodity's marketability, one factor is presented as crucial for any company's success, a point that is often supported by the use of metaphors, easy to understand and remember figures, as well as stylized examples or naïve exemplars, that is, narratives of successful cases in prominent organizations in which 'change is being grossly simplified' (Fincham, 1995: 711) but contribute to demonstrating a commodity's practical relevance (Clark and Greatbatch, 2004). In a similar way, theorists such as Furusten (1999) and Røvik (2002) conducted systematic analyses of popular ideas to uncover elements that enhance knowledge commodities' 'ability to flow' (Røvik, 2002: 114) such as social authorization, universalizing, commodification, timing, harmonizing, dramatizing, and individualizing.

Relatedly, an element highlighted by Berglund and Werr (2000) is that knowledge entrepreneurs not only use rhetorics to present their standardized knowledge products as objectified and universal, but also tend to emphasize the importance of an elaborate experience base in applying the knowledge commodity. In this way these entrepreneurs position themselves as 'obligatory passage points' (Berglund and Werr, 2000: 650) in the application of the management commodities they promote. This relates to Kieser's argument that 'the author points out that the concept is extremely difficult to implement so that many companies fail' (1997: 60). This means that knowledge entrepreneurs not only use rhetorical techniques to gain legitimacy for their solutions, but also to present themselves as indispensable in the effective implementation of their particular version of a commodity.

A second and related body of work has stressed that it is not only essential to study how the rhetoric used by knowledge entrepreneurs may convince management practitioners of the value of particular commodities, but also equally important is to consider how the form of these solutions may contribute to the managers' identity and role in contemporary organization (Jackson, 1996; Clark and Salaman, 1998; Jackson, 2001). As Clark and Salaman have argued, the way knowledge entrepreneurs present their commodities cannot solely be considered as purely transferring management knowledge to their clients, but should be seen as a means for: 'representing negotiated and mutually acceptable ways of knowing, defining and talking about management, organization and managers' (1998: 146). Thus, an important explanation for the perceived value of particular commodities constitutes the way in which they succeed in defining the managerial role, providing a rationale for their presence, and emphasizing their ability to shape the success of organizations. This relates to the assumed managers' need for self-esteem and their general concern in reducing the uncertainties and anxieties that pertain to managerial work (Huczynski, 1993: 171; Watson, 1994).

In line with this understanding, the work of Jackson (1996; 2001) identifies three main stages by which knowledge entrepreneurs may shape managers 'sense of themselves' to enhance the perceived value of their commodified forms of management knowledge. First, knowledge entrepreneurs tend to frighten managers by revealing a constellation of developments that constitute an immediate threat to the existence of their organization (Jackson, 1996; Benders and van Veen, 2001). Secondly, while creating a threatening picture for the near future of many organizations, Jackson (1996) noted that knowledge entrepreneurs also show empathy for the managers and stress their ability for change, for instance by showing examples of managers who have successfully coped with the specific problem situation. In this way they portray managers in heroic terms as the key actors or champions shaping the future of their organizations (Jackson, 1996). Finally, the 'new' managerial role is framed in relation to the knowledge commodity as the most efficient and innovative solution, thereby emphasizing the substantial personal rewards of putting efforts in realizing it (Jackson, 1996; ten Bos, 2000).

Third, a final and substantially growing strand of research has focused on the commodity's 'interpretative viability' as an important explanation of its perceived value and broad appeal among the managerial masses. This relates to the notion of linguistic ambiguity (Astley and Zammuto, 1992; Davis, 1986; Kieser, 1997) that is, 'the condition of admitting more than one meaning' (Giroux, 2006: 1232). Benders and van Veen (2001) explain that lending itself for different interpretation and usage allows a commodity to become perceived as valuable in a large variety of different situations. This may entail that a commodity is recognized and accepted by different parties because ambiguity of language within which a commodity is expressed may accommodate a multiplicity of divergent interests and preconceptions (Astley and Zammuto, 1992; Benders and van Veen, 2001). In addition, ambiguity allows resolving, or at least linguistically structuring, persistent and insoluble managerial issues or fundamentally irreconcilable events (Abrahamson, 1996; Berglund and Werr, 2000). As Astley and Zammuto argue: 'In the face of acute uncertainty and equivocality, ambiguous concepts ensure a measure of continuity by providing seemingly fixed points of reference which, in fact, are constantly reinterpreted in the process of adapting to change' (1992: 451).

While a commodity's linguistic ambiguity or 'interpretive viability' is considered an important element for its widespread acceptance among a managerial audience, theorists also emphasize that this also generates a number of challenges for research on the diffusion of knowledge commodities. A first issue is that given the possibility of different interpretations, it is 'impossible to judge the efficacy of a concept' (Benders and van Veen, 2001: 49). Indeed, despite the fact that commodified forms of management knowledge are often accompanied by substantial promises of performance improvements, the managers' perceptions of relative advantages may diverge significantly and may change over time (see for example Peters and Heusinkveld, 2010). Second, various authors have pointed to a positive feedback loop between ambiguity and popularity (Ansari et al., 2010; Benders and van Veen, 2001; Giroux, 2006). This entails that a commodity's ambiguity is not only an important condition to become popular, but is also affected by its popularity. In other words, a larger popularity creates a larger variety of different uses. This has engendered important debates about the elements that shape the interpretation and implementation of commodities (van Veen et al., 2011; Nicolai and Dautwiz, 2010; Zbaracki, 1998; Hackman and Wageman, 1995; Kelemen, 2000; Strang, 2010).

Process Approaches

Another important strand of work conceptualizes the generation and construction of new commodities by knowledge entrepreneurs as a series of distinct phases (Huczynski, 1993; Abrahamson, 1996; Suddaby and Greenwood, 2001), and particularly focuses on the steps in the conversion process of the knowledge itself (see Table 2.3).

In one of the earliest accounts, Huczynski (1993) takes a marketing perspective to examine the way management ideas are commodified and turned into a form capable of being marketed and sold. He identifies different states in the transformation of management ideas into successful products. A first state of a commodity-in-development that is identified by Huczynski involves 'raw material' (1993: 217). This 'raw material' may take the form of research findings, theories, principles, tips, or personal experiences, and are believed to constitute the basis for a new commodity, or in Huczynski's words: 'One can argue that the management wholesaler takes the raw material of the academic, consultant or hero-manager in a way similar to which a dairy product company buys bulk milk from a farmer. At this stage value is added and the products are destined for different markets' (1993: 217). A second major state identified by Huczynski (1993) involves various types of management ideas-based products: (a) teaching devices, (b) training events, (c) organizational development interventions, and (d) system-wide programs. It is emphasized that these types differ substantially in degree of 'structuralization', that is, their sophistication and possible implications for the client organization. Huczynski phrased this as follows: 'These four types of techniques are not equivalent, but represent progressively deeper and more permanent influences upon organizations' (1993: 214). He goes on by arguing that in order to become widely adopted each type has distinct implications for its marketing in terms of branding, advertising, and product development.

Table 2.3 Process approaches and their stages

Theorists	Perspective	Activities or stages				
Huczynski (1993)	*Marketing perspective*	Structuralization	Branding	Advertising	Product development	
Abrahamson (1996)	*Production of culture*	Creation	Selection	Processing	Dissemination	
Suddaby and Greenwood (2001)	*Institutional perspective*	Codification	Abstraction	Translation		
Birkinshaw et al. (2008)	*Evolutionary perspective*	Agenda setting	Idea linking	Idea testing	Theory linking	
Reihlen and Nikolova (2010)	*Self-organizing systems*	Integration	Professionalization	Mobilizing		

Another influential understanding of the process of commodification (Abrahamson, 1996; Abrahamson and Fairchild, 1999) draws on a conceptual model of cultural industries, as proposed by theorists such as Hirsch (1972) and Peterson (1979). These theorists assume 'a surplus of available raw material at the outset' (Hirsch, 1972: 649) and lay particular emphasis on the role of an 'industry system' in the filtering of potential new products and ideas before they arrive at the consumption stage. In line with this work, Abrahamson (1996) and Abrahamson and Fairchild (1999) conceptualize the process by which new knowledge commodities are produced as a series of four distinct phases. In an initial phase, knowledge suppliers seek to sense 'incipient preferences' (Abrahamson, 1996: 264) in a community of management knowledge consumers, thereby seeking to generate an inventory of potentially fruitful ideas. This is followed by a stage of selecting those managerial ideas that are believed to be marketable in the near future. In the processing stage, the ideas become formulated in such a way that presents them as a rational and progressive solution to contemporary organizational problems, or as Abrahamson phrases: 'fashion setters articulate the rhetorics championing the management techniques they select (1996: 264). During a final stage, the commodity is disseminated on the market for management solutions in order to become part of the managerial discourse, a central element in attracting the attention of knowledge consumers.

A third conceptualization of commodification draws on an institutional perspective to provide a field-level understanding of the processes that produce commodified forms of management knowledge (Suddaby and Greenwood, 2001; Clark, 2004; O'Mahoney et al., 2013). Here commodification is not considered an isolated or sole enterprise, but seen as a central part of broader recurrent patterns of creation, legitimation, and consumption of management knowledge. Indeed, it is assumed that these forms of management knowledge 'move cyclically between communities of actors within the organizational field' (Suddaby and Greenwood, 2001: 935). Within these recurrent cycles, commodification is conceptualized as comprising three essential processes. A first key process that is identified concerns the codification of localized, individual, and often tacit expertise. Converting such expertise into a form 'that can be stored, moved and reused' (Suddaby and Greenwood, 2001), is not only considered beneficial to other knowledge entrepreneurs, but also allows to establish 'property rights' (Morris, 2001: 821) to enhance one's business. Second, this codified raw material is then 'abstracted' into more structured and universal forms that allow it to be easily recognized as useful in a large variety of different organizational contexts and more readily deployed by other actors. Here theorists refer to structured methods that can take shape in a coherent cluster of step-approaches, frameworks, tools, and cases that are embedded in a specific language (Werr, 1999; Werr et al., 1997; Fincham and Evans, 1999). These codified approaches are not only seen as offering cognitive support to consultants in the advice process, but also as a means which allow consultants to reduce a client's and their own uncertainty about the trajectory in the problem-solving process (Werr and Stjernberg, 2003). Third, Suddaby and Greenwood (2001) emphasize that a final element of the knowledge production concerns the 'translation' of the abstracted repertoire and the 'reembedding' into a variety of different organizational contexts (see also Czarniawska and Sévon, 1996). This relates to the possibility to adapt the general ideas that are associated with that commodity to the specific client situation (Werr et al., 1997; Berglund and Werr, 2000; Werr and Stjernberg, 2003). As Benders, van den Berg, and van Bijsterveld (1998: 212) posit, consultants handle a management knowledge commodity 'highly pragmatically and tend to go along with customer demands and interpretations'. It is also emphasized in this literature that commodified forms of management knowledge do not directly shape the actions of consultants; rather it is 'improvisation' on these commodities that characterizes consultancy work (Morris, 2001; Furusten, 2009; Visscher and Fisscher, 2009).

A final and emerging stream of research sees commodification as a constellation of processes of collaborative social interaction between different actors. Theorists regard commodities as the outcome of active partnerships and cooperation within knowledge suppliers that operate on the 'backstage' (Clark and Greatbatch, 2002; 2004). For instance the study of Clark and Greatbatch (2004) shows that various people such as editors and ghostwriters have a significant impact on the process of commodification as they seek to collectively shape the initial ideas of (potential) management gurus in line with their specific beliefs of a successful knowledge product. As a result of these collaborative actions, the ideas are transformed significantly before they are launched as a new commodity on the market for management solutions.

Other scholars also emphasize the relevance of various external dimensions (Clark and Salaman, 1998; Birkinshaw et al., 2008; Reihlen and Nikolova, 2010). These studies stress the need to understand processes of knowledge commodification in terms of collaborative activities with external agents. For instance Clark and Salaman (1998) see guru-client interactions as essential elements in this process as it constitutes a source of new ideas and provides immediate feedback on a producer's knowledge products (see also Greatbatch and Clark, 2005). Reihlen and Nikolova's study (2010) extend this argument by explaining how consultants perform different activities such as those focused on integration, professionalization, and mobilization that shape interactions not only with the client, but also with the client firm's practice groups, their professional community, and the general public. It is suggested that the production of management knowledge is influenced significantly by the cognitive feedback that emerges from these interactions with many external 'collective actors'. In a similar vein, using an evolutionary perspective, Birkinshaw et al. (2008) defines four broad stages in the production of knowledge commodities and hypothesizes that, related to these stages, processes of agenda setting, idea linking, idea testing, and theory linking act as bridges between the divergent foci and occupational identities of relevant internal and external agents.

Evolutionary Approaches

A third broad and significant strand of work in the research on management knowledge commodification entails the way these commodities evolve once they are introduced on the market for managerial solutions. A key assumption that underlies most work involves that commodification of management knowledge stimulates the production of new commodities and the replacement of 'old' ideas. Providing a field-level analysis of the system of production and consumption of management knowledge, Suddaby and Greenwood (2001) present the commodification of management knowledge as a cyclical and institutionalized process between different knowledge market actors. These actors' interactions continuously induce recurrent patterns of knowledge creation, legitimation, and consumption. Congruent to the view of earlier accounts such as from Huczynski (1993) they argue that converting management knowledge into a commoditized form 'produces a spiraling need for new ideas and managerial practices that can be commodified and sold' (2001: 945).

Accounts of various commentators indicate that management intellectuals and practitioners have always been repeatedly confronted with allegedly innovative management ideas. Already in 1956, Bendix noted: 'At several points the [preceding] discussion of the American experience has suggested that ideologies are reiterated endlessly and are essentially ambiguous. [. . .] Both the ambiguity of ideologies and the lack of personal involvement often provide an opening wedge for new ideas, or at least new emphases' (1956: 342). Also other widely renowned work includes incidental observations. For instance Joan Woodward is well known in organization studies for her typology of technical systems in relation to the characteristics of the products they produce. What is less known, however, is that she also observed that the many changes in the managerial ideas defined the shape of changes in organizations: 'Management fashion also had an important part in organizational changes. The urge to 'keep up with the Joneses' seems to be as powerful a force in industrial circles as in social life.' (1965: 22). Similarly, Lawrence and Lorsch have become widely recognized for their research on contingency theory, but something that is edited out of the collective knowledge on this research is their observation about the cycles in the supply of new managerial ideas: 'The last fifty years of executive life have been filled with a multitude of important new methods and techniques for running a business. Around the turn of the century business was being urged to systematize in terms of cost accounting, production control and budgeting. Then the Scientific Management movement came in, with time and motion studies and job and workflow rationalization. About the same time a plethora of monetary incentive systems, such as the infamous Bedeaux plan came into vogue' (1967: 160).

Although the above examples indicate that recurring cycles on management knowledge market have long been noted, it was not until the early 1990s that this phenomenon received systematic attention from management theorists. In these early theorizations, the evolution of new knowledge commodities is primarily conceptualized as a bell-shaped pattern in which a rapid growth in popularity is quickly followed by a sharp decline. Using a marketing perspective, Huczynski (1993) argued that, like any product, knowledge commodities go through a life cycle and identified different stages including introduction, growth, maturity, saturation, and decline. Moreover by discussing the typical motives of managers as 'consumers' and consultants as 'producers' Huczynski explained how '. . . the cycle of management fads will continue to be with us in for the foreseeable future' (1993: 268). In a similar vein, based on an analysis of the evolution of three management ideas (Management by Objectives, Organization Development, and Total Quality Management) Gill and Whittle (1993) typified four distinct phases through which knowledge commodities tend to proceed, and sought to explain these cyclical patterns in managerial activity by emphasizing the role of cultural and psychodynamic factors. Gill and Whittle (1993) argue that, typically, a birth phase in the evolution of these consultant-driven approaches, in which a guru-in-development transforms management knowledge into a saleable form, is followed by a period of rapid growth indicating an increasing enthusiasm for the commodity among other knowledge entrepreneurs. After a short phase of maturity characterized by further routinization of the repertoire of these knowledge entrepreneurs, a phase of decline sets in when the management knowledge commodity cannot meet its initial expectations, is no longer regarded as innovative, and is faced with newer and more promising solutions. Also the understanding of Abrahamson (1996) emphasizes the short-lived and noncumulative nature of commodities' impact that is shaped by knowledge entrepreneurs.

The commonly held thesis that the evolution of management knowledge commodities resembles a bell-shaped curve has been empirically examined and assessed by various studies (Pascale, 1990; Abrahamson and Fairchild, 1999; Carson et al., 1999; Jones and Thwaites, 2000; Heusinkveld and Benders, 2001; Scarbrough and Swan, 2001; Giroux, 2006). Most of these studies base themselves on more or less elaborate analyses of print media data (Clark, 2004; Benders et al., 2007). In line with these prior theories, these studies revealed generic short lived bell-shaped patterns in the discourse on different knowledge commodities. In addition, studies related the distinct phases in the intensity of discourse to the evolution in the tenor of this discourse (Abrahamson and Fairchild, 1999; Jones and Thwaites, 2000; Benders and van Veen, 2001). For instance, Abrahamson and Fairchild (1999) found that the increasing media attention for Quality Circles (QC) in the early 1980s was paralleled by positive evaluations and high expectations about the possibility of performance improvement in the market. In contrast, the study revealed that increasing negative evaluations and a more critical attitude to the idea paralleled the downswing in media discourse on

QC. It is suggested that after a period of excitement and high enthusiasm, a management idea inevitably becomes increasingly criticized and loses its initial image of rationality and progress.

Giroux (2006) provided a similar explanation for the assumed short-lived and noncumulative patterns. On the basis of a study of the way guru texts on Total Quality Management (TQM) evolved she suggests that, as they grow on popularity, knowledge commodities become: 'more ambiguous, vaguer and more encompassing' (Giroux, 2006: 1254; see also Ansari et al., 2010; Cole, 1999). Relatedly, Hackman and Wageman concluded on the evolution of TQM that: 'An astonishing number of other interventions, some related to TQM and some not, are increasingly being herded under the TQM banner' (1995: 338). Also other theorists noted that from a 'reasonably well-defined and established technical intervention' TQM became 'an ambiguous and sometimes dubious intervention' (Zbaracki, 1998: 603; see also Hackman and Wageman, 1995; Kelemen, 2000). In the process of putting TQM to use in U.S. organizations, TQM was broadened from statistical process control to an overall managerial approach to 'manage quality' which was drawn upon selectively when implementing TQM.

Over the years, this research had engendered different debates around the evolving dynamics of particular knowledge commodities. First, various theorists have emphasized the need to nuance and further develop prior conceptualization in different ways. For instance Abrahamson and Fairchild (1999) hypothesized that popular commodities do not emerge out of nowhere. Rather, their research indicated that, similar to cultural artifacts that may reside in specific subcultures, a dormancy phase involving a relatively long period of little attention tend to precede a short-lived popularity wave. Also some theorists indicate that, in time, the life span of commodities tend to shorten and their intensity is getting higher (Pascale, 1990; Kieser, 1997; Carson et al., 1999). Moreover, analyses of commodities' evolution pattern not only furthered understanding concerning their longevity (Carson et al., 1999; Braam et al., 2007) but also have pointed to important variations between the evolution of commodities between different discursive fields. For instance Benders and van Bijsterveld (2000) were able to show that the general shape of discourse intensity about Lean Production (LP) was characterized by a sinusoid wave during the 1990s. However, as indicated by further analysis, LP became particularly popular in Germany during this time period while in many other countries the idea was hardly discussed. In addition, content analyses showed that the way LP was interpreted in the German discourse differed significantly not only from the original LP practices at Toyota Motors, but also from the book *The Machine that Changed the World*, generally considered as the most important text on LP.

Other studies provided an enhanced understanding into how various professional groups may shape the extent and way a commodity is received and interpreted (Heusinkveld and Benders, 2001; Scarbrough and Swan, 2001; Braam et al., 2007). For instance studying the evolution of the discourse on

Knowledge Management (KM) Scarbrough and Swan concluded that: 'The enthusiastic championing of KM by the IS community can be contrasted with the somewhat belated reaction of Personnel or Human Resources specialists' (2001: 10). The studies of Heusinkveld and Benders (2001) and Braam et al. (2007) did not only show important differences in the intensity of discourse on a particular commodity between different professional communities, but also indicated variety in interpretation and longevity. For instance while in most professional communities the initial large attention to BPR seems to fade away towards the end of the 1990s, Heusinkveld and Benders' study indicated that: 'The IS community shows strong bases that increase the likelihood of entrenchment' (2001: 247). Thus the above research work particularly emphasizes the importance of considering the specific context in which a commodity emerges and defining these boundaries in understanding a commodity's evolution.

A second broad area of discussion around the life cycle thesis relates to the notion of coevolution. Indeed, the life cycle conceptualization suggests that a commodity's up- and downswing in discourse strongly relates to its adoption in organizational praxis. In support of this understanding Abrahamson and Fairchild (1999) reported that the upsurge in articles on Quality Circles (QC) in the U.S. during the early 1980s coincided with an increase in adoption of the label among a large number of U.S. firms. They found indications that the unfavorable tenor and downswing of discourse in the business media during the mid-1980s reinforced large-scale rejection of the QC label across populations of companies (Abrahamson and Fairchild, 1999: 732). In a similar way, David and Strang (2006) demonstrated how consultancies went into the market for TQM by adopting its label when this management idea was becoming fashionable in the early 1980s. While after the boom, they withdrew by not using the label, thereby leaving TQM once again to a small number of specialists. At the same time a number of theorists have criticized the assumed 'relationship' between the evolving dynamics in the print media discourse and the adoption and implementation of knowledge commodities by organizations. In an early account, Bendix (1956) expressed that there is no doubt about the occurrence of changes in organizational practices in relation to the prevalence of particular 'management ideologies' in the wider managerial discourse, but emphasized that these are easily overestimated. Rather, Bendix sees the changes associated with these ideologies as: 'gradual and ambiguous, for the old ideas have been rephrased rather than abandoned' (1956: 339).

More recently, Clark developed a critique on the assumed coevolutionary, or 'symbiotic relationship' (2004: 299) between discourse and practice by discussing the possibilities and limitations of the widely used print media analyses and emphasizing that future research need to focus more on 'understanding the nature and process by which organizations adopt fashionable management ideas' (2004: 304). In line with these critiques, the study of Nijholt and Benders (2007) revealed important trends in the prevalence of Self-Managing Teams (SMT) in praxis over time in relation to patterns in the volume of print media discourse. Drawing on different sources of trend data studying the number of organizations that use SMT over time in a more rhetorical and substantive sense this paper not only provides support for the assertion that: 'trends in discourse are not necessarily indicative of trends in the application of organization concepts in praxis' (2007: 22), but also pointed to significant difficulties of measurement and importance of using multiple and sometimes incompatible sources to address these difficulties.

A third and important debate related to the life cycle thesis concerns the way management knowledge commodities may or may not survive a fashion boom and bust. While some accounts particularly focus on transitory elements in the evolution of knowledge commodities (Gill and Whittle, 1993 Abrahamson, 1996), others emphasize the elements that may signify or enhance the likelihood of entrenchment (Zeitz et al., 1999) or 'long-term viability' (Stjernberg and Philips, 1993). Indeed, various studies indicate that actors may keep using a fashionable management idea even though the label may no longer be in vogue among management intellectuals (Marchington et al., 1993; Guillén, 1994; Beck and Walgenbach, 2005; Nijholt and Benders, 2007; O'Mahoney, 2007). For example, while the managerial discourse on ISO 9000 gradually silenced and the management idea became increasingly criticized for reducing the flexibility of organizations, empirical evidence shows that in organizational praxis '. . . the standards have become increasingly institutionalized' (Beck and Walgenbach, 2005: 844). In a similar way Cole (1999) argued that the decrease in the use of TQM language coincided with organizations actually 'doing' it. His longitudinal analysis of TQM experiences at Hewlett Packard showed that the practices initially associated with the TQM language remained as 'building blocks' (1999: 235) for new initiatives. These institutionalized practices may even be drawn upon and revisited in new change initiatives (Røvik, 1996; De-Cock and Hipkin, 1997; Benders, 1999; Easton and Jarrell, 2000).

Building on this research, the study of Perkmann and Spicer (2008) has explored the possibility that once fashionable knowledge commodities 'acquire permanence' (2008: 812), and in particular the conditions under which this may take place. Drawing on the notion of 'institutional work' they identified various forms of institutional entrepreneurship that are directly related to one of the institutional pillars (Scott, 2001) such as political work, technical work, and cultural work as important factors that increase the likelihood of institutionalization of fashions. Similarly, drawing on the notion of sedimentation, Røvik argued that former popular management ideas may resist the pressure for change so that 'prescriptions that have become obsolete may have become very entrenched in organizations' (1996: 163; see also Heusinkveld and Benders, 2012). It is argued that entrenched knowledge commodities do not only take shape as changes in tasks or management systems, but may also remain in the memory of the people involved in an approach's introduction and implementation or may reside in established training programs. Theorists of organizational evolution even argued that present organizations retain important 'traces' that were implemented as from their time of origin. These traces remain latent until they are explicitly recalled in later phases (Stinchcombe, 1965; O'Mahoney, 2007).

A fourth and final substantial strand of theorizing can be subsumed under the 'old wine in new bottles' view. A number of different theorists note repeatedly that management knowledge commodities presented as 'new' actually may contain substantial reiterations of existing ideas (Barley and Kunda, 1992; Bendix, 1956; Jacques, 1996; Kieser, 1996; Lammers, 1988; Spell, 2001). These accounts suggest more continuity, or at least more gradual changes, in the evolution of management knowledge than the rapid turnover of new commodities would suggest (Abrahamson and Eisenman, 2008; Lammers, 1988; Spell, 2001). For instance, in one of the earlier accounts Bendix observed that old ideas have been rephrased in a new language in order to gain widespread acceptance, or in his words: 'traditional ideologies have been formulated anew in the terminology which have been currently fashionable' (1956: 342). Building on this seminal work of Bendix, Guillén (1994) posited that the history of organizational analysis should be interpreted in terms of the three basic approaches of organization and management. He observed that important elements of these approaches that were established in the early 20th century are incorporated in both the ideology and the underlying techniques of dominant management ideas of the 1990s such as Lean Production (LP) and TQM. Similarly, Huczynski (1993) argued that new commodities are to be seen as variations of six foundational families of managerial thinking, i.e. Bureaucracy, Scientific Management, Administrative Theory, Human Relations, Neo Human Relations, and Guru Theory. Overall, these accounts generally imply that, despite what the continuous emergence of 'new' commodities would suggest, what is presented as novel does not necessarily differ so much from the 'old'.

The above observations have urged some scholars to warn against the danger of reinventing the wheel and the underutilization of current organizational knowledge (Lammers, 1988; Jacques, 1996). In the words of the renowned sociologist Cornelis Lammers, the problem is not so much the 'continuity' of specific 'old' insights, but 'the lack of accumulation' (1988: 219). Lammers' critical analysis of the contemporary popular idea Excellent Organizations, as presented in the early 1980s by Peters and Waterman, indicated that similar insights have emerged incessantly in literature, only from different research traditions and under different labels (Lammers, 1988). German sociologists in the 1920s and 1930s already wrote about nonhierarchical organizations with a low degree of formalization. Also in following decades variations on the same ideas were put forward. Moreover, Lammers (1986) found that the authors of the management best seller *In Search of Excellence* not only reproduced old knowledge without referring to earlier sources, but also used inadequate research methods. However, at the same time he argues about these authors that: 'In sum, they should not have done it in this way but I am very glad they *did* it' (1986: 27), hereby pointing at the fact that the book made no contribution to management knowledge *an sich* but caused that management thinking about the subject received a new impetus among both management practitioners and management scholars (Barley et al., 1988).

In line with this, ten Bos (2000) argues that fashionable commodities may inspire managers with 'new' ideas, but at the same time noted that a key element that persists in management fashion is that, by their inherent focus on novelty and progress, they tend to obliterate the past and therefore are condemned to repeat it. He even marks that 'forgetfulness is a defining characteristic of the utopian mind' (2000: 175) indicating that a permanent inability to systematically build on existing insights and experiences means that people have to reinvent what others already knew and repeat the same basic mistakes, or as Benders and Vermeulen phrase: '. . . developing yet other tools is not the sole solution and perhaps even part of the larger problem' (2002: 164). In a similar way Jacques (1996) emphasized that reiterating management knowledge without cumulatively building on previous experiences leads to an important problem that people lose sight of an idea's origin and its related cultural and historical roots (see also Shenhav, 1999; Grint and Case, 1998).

Theorists have provided various explanations for the 'old wine in new bottles' phenomenon. Some stress that reiterating 'old' solutions likely occurs at a large scale because of pendulum swings in trying to solve basically insoluble organizational dilemmas such as centralization-decentralization and specialization-diversification (Nicolai and Thomas, 2006). Ramsay (1977, in Sturdy, 2004) argues that these swings are the inevitable product of the contradictions inherent in the capitalist mode of organizing. Based on historical data, various studies identified specific periods in which a particular management idea or approach dominated management thinking. Some explanations argue that macroeconomic waves shape, at least to some extent, what management knowledge producers and consumers think and do (Barley and Kunda, 1992; Abrahamson, 1997). Other theorists provide more volitional explanations by hypothesizing that the re-emergence of specific ideas and ideologies is influenced by more general changes in intellectual climate (Eastman and Bailey, 1998) or wider problems in the contemporary society (Nelson, 1975; Shenhav, 1999).

More recently, Abrahamson and Eisenman (2008) suggested that while the vocabulary of new commodities may differ from its predecessors, thereby creating as sense of novelty and progress, they also share important similarities in terms of contents. Because of this overlap, consecutive commodities should be considered as part of larger trends implying that they 'connect and cumulate rather than constituting individual and unpredictable responses' (2008: 725). As Ortmann (1995) has pointed out, continuously introducing new knowledge products makes the existing regarded as old and less attractive while at the same time the 'old' should be considered constitutive for what can be regarded as 'new'. But how the 'new' collides with the 'old' in organizational praxis still remains largely unexplored, and is not an uncomplicated issue or as Watson suggests: '. . . the pattern that is left is rarely a neat one and it is never predictable' (1986: 47).

THE RESEARCH

To address the central concern in this book, I collected three types of data: (1) print media publications authored by management consultants, (2) in-depth interviews with these management consultants, and (3) case data of more and less successful commodification ventures in different consultancies. These different methods and multiple data sources offered us an opportunity to create a richer view of the way the social life of commodified forms of management knowledge is perceived and shaped. Moreover, the print media publications allow us to verify the data collected through the interviews, as these publications are immune to retrospective modifications. We discuss the three types of data in more detail below.

Print Media Indicators

To get a better insight into the way knowledge commodities are developed and advocated by management consultants I focused on focus on Business Process Reengineering (BPR), a management idea that already has experienced major changes in popularity (Benders and van Veen, 2001; Carson et al., 1999). Hammer and Champy's (1993) work *Reengineering the Corporation,* commonly regarded as the main BPR text, is seen as 'the biggest selling business book of the 1990s' (Jackson, 1996: 575). In addition to its widespread managerial popularity, BPR has been added to the service portfolios of many consultancies (Benders et al., 1998; Fincham, 1995; Fincham and Evans, 1999; O'Shea and Madigan, 1997). At the time of the data collection, BPR had moved well past its prime popularity (Carson et al., 1999; Heusinkveld and Benders, 2001), providing us a theoretically relevant opportunity to study how consultants deal with this situation.

I started by scanning print media publications on BPR as important outlets for consultants' knowledge products (Faust, 2002; Braam et al., 2007). These publications not only allow further promotion of their services, but also provide an opportunity for consultants' proprietary claims as the key supplier of a new commodity (Fincham, 1995; Morris, 2001). Following a common method to investigate a management knowledge commodity's evolving popularity (Benders et al., 2007) I searched the Dutch-language bibliographic databases OnLine Contents, KUB Online Contents, Excerpta Informatica, and Management CD using the keywords 'reengineering, 'BPR', and 'process redesign' (see Heusinkveld and Benders, 2001). In line with Guillén (1994), I focused on BPR in a single country, the Netherlands, to ensure that I developed a comprehensive view of a market for a particular commodity in one lingual context. Moreover, choosing this particular context related to the authors' in-depth knowledge of the specific institutional setting which provided opportunities in finding theoretically relevant informants, gaining their support, and interpreting and comparing the data. In addition, the general life cycle of discourse about BPR in the Netherlands is consistent with its international evolution (Abrahamson and Fairchild, 1999; Heusinkveld and Benders, 2001; Kieser, 1997).

After gaining an initial overview of who was active in the BPR market on the basis of BPR publications, I concentrated on a sample of consultants who were closely involved in the development, supply, and implementation of BPR and who agreed to participate in the research. Subsequently, I not only focused on the BPR articles published by these consultants, but also searched for new publications and commercial material from these selected consultants that appeared after the BPR discourse had faded. This search revealed that, after the BPR hype, the consultants not only wrote about new topics such as Balanced Scorecard (BSC), Straight Through Processing (STP), Mergers, and E-business, but also published about their ideas in new fields. In the end, our search for print media publications resulted in a sample of 49 books and articles authored by management consultants comprising 814 pages of text (Appendix II). The publications show that the consultants started publishing on BPR in different years and appeared within journals and magazines focused on different functional fields such as General Management, Accounting, IT, and Health care Management. Also, while some consultants published a single piece on this topic, others appeared in professional media more regularly or were not involved in publishing at all.

Interview Data

In addition to using the Dutch print media data discussed above, I conducted a series of interviews with the 44 consultants from 24 different firms (see Appendix I); the focus was on the specific role of management ideas in the broader daily work of these consultants. As indicated, the key criterion in the composition of the theoretical sample was that all consultants were closely involved in the development of a new commodity within their firm and most of them published about it in a book or professional magazine. Where possible, I invited different consultants from the same consultancy to obtain multiple views of the development process. Also two consultants were interviewed about their role in different consultancies (E1 = L2 and O1 = X1). Overall, the informants varied in their hierarchical levels (partner, managing consultant, senior consultant, and junior consultant) and the firms varied significantly in origin, size, and background (see Appendix I). By maximizing the variety of different settings I sought to obtain a richer view of the elements that play a role in the commodification process, thereby enhancing the likelihood of further densification in the emergent theory (Glaser and Strauss, 1967; Wester, 1995; Strauss and Corbin, 1998). While I interviewed mainly Dutch consultants, the headquarters of their firms were located in the Netherlands, the United States, the United Kingdom, and France. The size of the consultancies or their subsidiaries ranged from three to more than several thousand consultants. The main practice areas of these informants covered a wide spectrum of areas, including change management, IT implementation, IT strategy, strategic management, personnel management, health care management, financial management, performance management, and industrial management.

I conducted semistructured interviews in which the respondents were asked to describe the entire process of commodification in relation to a particular case in their consultancy. The interviews covered several key themes that directly related to a management idea's social life: (1) the introduction, (2) the uptake, and (3) the development in time. In these interviews, the attention was not only on the way consultants adopt 'new' management ideas, but particularly on their experiences with these ideas on the market and within client organizations. This implied that the interviewees were asked to discuss the perceived changes to the commodity over time, and how they frame these commodities as enacted practices in the context of a client-organization and why they did it in this way. Depending on the experience of the consultant, I was able to ask more detailed questions as the interviews progressed. Interviews were held at the consultancies' offices and on average lasted about 90 minutes (minimum of 60 minutes). All interviews were recorded on minidisk, transcribed, and returned to the respondents for comments.

Case-study Data

In further enhancing the development of a more holistic view of management knowledge commodification, I undertook a more in-depth analysis of two cases of new concept development ventures within different consultancies. The first case involved an ultimately successful yet somewhat 'bumpy' commodification project in a reasonably large consultancy and was studied in detail. This means that quite a few barriers had to be overcome before the new commodity was launched, which is probably much more typical for a development project than the average success story which makes it to publication. The case organization, DCE Consulting, is an international consultancy firm employing about 250 consultants located in offices in Belgium, the Netherlands, United Kingdom, France, and Luxembourg at the time of study. Since 1997, DCE is part of an international stock exchange-listed group of high-tech consultancies. The consultancy is structured into a matrix. Most consultants work in the market groups Trade and Industry, Energy and Utilities, Telecom and Media, Financial Services, Public Sector, and Health care. Furthermore, expertise groups, also dubbed as Centers of Excellence (CoE) coordinate the development and management of the 'knowledge products'. At the moment of the study the firm had four CoEs with three or four employees each. These cover their range of services: IT Management, Change Management, Process Management, and as a new area, Marketing Management.

The description is primarily based on an insider account of one of the interviewees from the above sample. As senior consultant, he was involved in the project from its conception to the launch and application in client organizations. This position in the organization allowed privileged access to data of various natures, such as project documentation, e-mails, presentations, flyers, client offers, internal correspondence, and insider views over a longer period of time. In addition, the project could be documented over its whole lifetime, that is, more than two years. The longitudinal approach and elaborate access to data are important advantages over case studies solely conducted by external researcher(s). However, our approach obviously entails the risk of an overly positive and merely personal account. To compensate for that, various documentary sources were made available to the other authors, and more importantly, I had been in contact with the firm at an earlier stage as an external researcher. The starting point was an internal lecture, held for the consultants. This was followed up by several interviews with the main 'concept champion' and my key informant. The position as an external researcher enabled me to gather data and opinions from other informants to validate our description.

The second case focused on the development of a commodity Product-Based Design (PBD) (Reijers et al., 2003) venture in another consultancy from the original sample. PBD is considered a methodology that can be used to develop efficient designs for highly information-intensive business processes, as they are typically found in the service industry and have been primarily promoted under the label of BPR. Unlike the first case, efforts of the consultants involved ultimately did not result in gaining 'good currency' for the venture and its underlying design method even though PBD was implemented and invariably led to significant benefits for the organizations in question. So in spite of PBD's technical performance, the commodification efforts decreased which eventually tarnished the viability of the method, as can be noted from the limited use of this method in recent projects. Rather than becoming further institutionalized, the development of this design methodology has 'quietly died'.

The PBD methodology has been a coproduction between Eindhoven University of Technology (EUT) and the Dutch branch of one of the world's largest accounting and consultancy firms employing more than 20,000 people worldwide. The Dutch branch included about 300 consultants and particularly focused on Strategy Consulting, Interim Management, and ICT Consulting. The area of ICT Consulting comprised two main practice areas, namely Architecture and Business Process Management. In terms of sectors, ICT Consulting was particularly active in Financial Services, Government Agencies, and Transport & Logistics.

For the analysis I drew from rich sources of material to describe the initiation, development, and consequent stagnation of PBD. This material consists of about 100 e-mails, presentations and various documents concerning the PBD method, such as commercial client offerings, reports of assignments, and internal project proposals. The description is also based on participant observations and iterative rounds of sensemaking during the development process. The role of an integral and active participant allowed for all commodification activities to be accessible. It also provided important possibilities of revealing key elements in the way the commodification venture is experienced, an area which has been unexplored in the literature. In addition, I held ex-post interviews with the four most involved developers. These were transcribed and authorized by the interviewees. In the case description, I particularly focus on the problems that were encountered by the consultants in legitimizing their approach after its initial successful application.

3   Sensing the Market

In the previous chapters I have emphasized that a large number of 'new' management ideas succeeded in gaining a resounding effect on the managerial masses and that this occurred for a large part through the productivization or commodification efforts of knowledge entrepreneurs such as management consultants and management gurus. It is argued that these knowledge entrepreneurs have a special talent that allows them to keep in tune with managerial demand. For instance, Jackson noted that 'the reason management gurus are so popular with practicing managers is that they recognize, understand and cater to their needs and preoccupations' (1996: 572). It is assumed that knowledge entrepreneurs seek to 'sense incipient preferences' among their potential clients before selecting, processing, and disseminating their ideas (Abrahamson, 1996). Critical accounts even suggest that these entrepreneurs simultaneously feed these needs by reinforcing and playing upon managers' anxiety, uncertainty, and fear of losing control in various ways (Sturdy, 1997).

An established stream of research has emphasized the importance of interactive processes in the production of management ideas in which client should be seen as cocreators (Huczynski, 1993: 258; Fosstenløken et al., 2003). Management guru Eliyahu Goltratt provided a telling example of this client participation when he explained to his audience that they 'sold' his Theory of Constraints to themselves (Oliver, 1990: 25, cited in Huczynski, 1993). Indeed, Clark and Greatbatch (2002) pointed out a guru's performance is not only to present new ideas, but also is particularly seen as an opportunity to test them. Gurus seek to elicit responses from the audience on their ideas in various ways: they are telling stories, inviting laughter by using humor (Greatbatch and Clark, 2005), or drawing on claptraps (Huczynski, 1993: 261). As a result, the audience ultimately contributes to the message they will receive, sometimes by speaking to the guru, and in other occasions by nonverbal responses. Thus, while we know more about the importance of interaction between 'innovator' and consumer, little is known about how the results of such 'sensing processes' are translated into new commodities that can be readily sold on the market for management solutions (Huczynski, 1993; Suddaby and Greenwood, 2001).

To address this issue, this chapter explores the process by which management consultants acquire, interpret, and utilize client information in the context of new management knowledge commodification ventures. I draw on the market orientation literature because it provides an understanding of how customer needs play a role in innovation processes (Deshpande and Zaltman, 1982; Kohli and Jaworski, 1990; Brown and Ennew, 1995; Adams et al., 1998; Kok et al., 2003) and how this is considered crucial to the success of a new product (Garrone and Colombo, 1999; Orihata and Watanabe, 2000). These elements are still underdeveloped in the current literature on the supply-side dynamics of management ideas. Using longitudinal case study data, I argue in this chapter that the market sensing process is not considered as a single inquiry into contemporary managerial needs. Rather, translating client information into new commodified forms of knowledge is related to the ability to 'orchestrate' the constant interaction of elements both external and internal to the consultancy and involves (1) continuously performing market information processing activities throughout the entire development process, and requires (2) internal organizational capabilities that enable learning about clients. Revealing various key elements that may enhance or inhibit consultants' development process of new forms of commodified knowledge allows us to develop a better understanding of the way knowledge entrepreneurs seek to remain in tune with market demand and are able to appeal to the managerial masses.

MARKET ORIENTATION

The current literature on management knowledge commodification discussed in earlier chapters shows the various relevant stages in translating management knowledge into a marketable product. In this section I further explore how the process of market sensing takes shape in relation to the process of management idea production particularly in management consultancies by drawing on the literature on market sensing. In other words, how exactly do knowledge entrepreneurs seek to sense the managerial needs and translate this information into new service offerings? I discuss the importance of (1) the constant gathering and processing of market data, and (2) the internal organizational capabilities to perform these processes.

Market Information Processing

Marketing theorists stress the importance of continuous learning about customers. This learning process involves a series of information processing activities (Day, 1994), that is, generating, distributing, and interpreting clients' needs, responses, and environmental trends. Thus, market sensing is considered not an isolated activity at the start of a development project, but relevant in every phase of the new product development process

(Kok et al., 2003). A first constellation of activities related to market sensing involves the continuous generation of data about customers' needs and
about wider environmental developments from various sources. The nature
of this information may vary in every stage of the development process.
However, it is indicated that information on clients and their reaction to
new products is inherently ambiguous (Adams et al., 1998). Clients' needs
may not be articulated clearly and may be subject to change. Such ambiguities and changes are likely to feed different opinions and controversies about
what clients actually need.

A second central activity entails the dissemination of the generated market information across different organizational functions through both formal and informal networks. Market information is not necessarily shared
quickly across different boundaries. The generation and application of
market knowledge is typically allocated to different people or units, spa-
tially separated and characterized by different orientations and structures.
The dissemination of market information may be hampered because different groups lack the ability to recognize the value of this new information
(Cohen and Levinthal, 1990) or are unwilling to appreciate and use knowledge from outside (Szulanski, 1996).

Finally, during all phases, the information requires interpretation through
'sorting, classification and simplification' (Day, 1994: 43) which are shaped
by organizational members' mental models and political interests (Brown
and Ennew, 1995; Jones and Stevens, 1999). This interpretation constitutes
the basis for decision making about the way ideas can be transformed into a
successful product. However, in line with theorists of organizational knowing, it is likely that new information is not automatically recognized as useful or utilized in organizations (Tsoukas, 1996; Orlikowski, 2002).

Organizational Capabilities

Market sensing activities are made possible by an organization's internal
capabilities to understand, process, and use this information (Kok et al.,
2003). As discussed, some barriers hamper the process of generation, dissemination, and utilization of market information within organizations,
thereby impeding the process of market learning. Consequently, organizational capabilities define how information processing activities are shaped,
thus determining the organizational ability to deal with tensions and overcome potential barriers (Cohen and Levinthal, 1990; Doughterty, 1996;
Vermeulen, 2005). This means that the ways market intelligence is translated into action and gains 'good currency' (van de Ven, 1986) may differ
significantly across firms.

The first crucial aspect concerns the commitment of senior management. Such a commitment requires a willingness to take risk and 'accept
occasional failures as being natural' (Kohli and Jaworski, 1990: 8). The
new product development literature shows that established organizational

routines are often unable to accommodate innovative activities and cause difficulties in dealing with the uncertainties and changes associated with developing new ideas (Dougherty and Heller, 1994). As Burns and Stalker noted, the strength of the political system and existing 'status structure' tend to confirm the status quo within an organization (1961: 126). A committed management attitude fosters a climate in which organizational members are likely to develop and implement new ideas.

A second key element that may enhance an organizational capability for market sensing is related to interdepartmental dynamics. It is argued that a strong connectedness and a lack of conflict between different departments within an organization enhance the dissemination of relevant market information (Kohli and Jaworski, 1990; Kok et al., 2003). In addition, the utilization of this market information is related to the receptivity of departments to this information. New ideas may violate existing departmental practices or may be 'unthinkable' in the light of their current institutionalized thought structure (Dougherty and Heller, 1994). However, as Kohli and Jaworski (1990) argue, the 'concern for others' ideas' may increase the behavioral impact of market intelligence on other departments, thereby enhancing an organization's market orientation. Thus, the literature on market sensing also points to the importance of internal organizational conditions for the utilization of client information in new product development (Deshpande and Zaltman, 1982).

THE PROCESSES AND CONSEQUENCES OF MARKET SENSING

To illustrate how market sensing issues play a crucial role in the commodification of management knowledge, I discuss the case of a commodification venture: Marketing Excellence. In the following sections I draw from rich sources of material to describe the precipitating arrangements and initiation, development impact of this management idea in DCE consulting, an international consultancy firm employing about 250 consultants at the time of study. According to the firm's strategy, consultants can contribute to the development and introduction of new management ideas in two different ways. First, consultants can actively participate in so-called Service Groups concentrating on the development of new management ideas under the supervision of a CoE manager. Each service group has a champion who is often the initiator of the new idea and holds important expertise on the subject. Consultants from different market sectors supplement this group. These consultants further develop the innovation and constitute a 'linking pin' to their own market group. In some cases, the knowledge 'products' developed by the CoE are adapted and are tailored to the characteristics of the specific market sector. The intensive collaboration with clients during the commodification process is meant to ensure that only potentially successful 'products' are developed. At the same time, the CoE manager remains in charge of the adapted management ideas, and assesses whether the services are applied correctly by the different market sectors. This means that the manager reviews offers and presentations of a market group before they are offered to clients.

The second way is by being involved in Business Development, that is, the introduction of new 'products' at extant and potential clients often in a particular sector (Fincham et al., 2008). Business Development is more focused on the commercial aspects of the commodification process, i.e. the introduction of new management ideas in the market and within client organizations. The activities that can be undertaken are for instance talking with potential clients, organizing roundtable discussions with clients, presenting during seminars, publishing in professional magazines, and sending commercial mailings. By these activities, new forms of commodified management knowledge are disseminated on the market and likely generate new ideas for further development. The feedback that is induced by these business development activities provides important input for enhancing a consultancy's current 'knowledge products'.

The commodification process is led by the annual CoE plan. The main issues for development are determined in dialogue with the different market groups within DCE and the market itself. The process starts with the construction of an overview of the requested 'products' and a plan for their development. In an initial stage the ideas for development merely concern 'rumors'. After approval by the general management, a project team is formed to construct the new 'product'. Below I provide an elaborate account of the evolution of a new management idea within DCE consulting: Marketing Excellence (see Table 3.1).

Champions and Market Needs

The idea for a new service in the field of marketing originated from two consultants. Both had a background in marketing and were interested in commodifying and applying these marketing issues in their client work. They felt that the organization and development of the marketing function in client organizations received little attention on the market for management solutions. Conversations with different clients confirmed these embryonic ideas and reinforced the notion that a new approach that concentrates on improving the performance of an organization's internal marketing activities could be considered valuable by clients. These initial ideas were written down in a presentation to the management of the consultancy. Subsequently, the initiators or 'concept champions' worked out an initial description of the management knowledge commodity, and a development plan in an internal document that included an elaboration of issues such as: what is Marketing Excellence? What are the current problems and solutions on the market? What is the business relevance? What is the business opportunity for DCE? What knowledge elements already exist within DCE and what services should be developed?

Table 3.1 Processes of market sensing

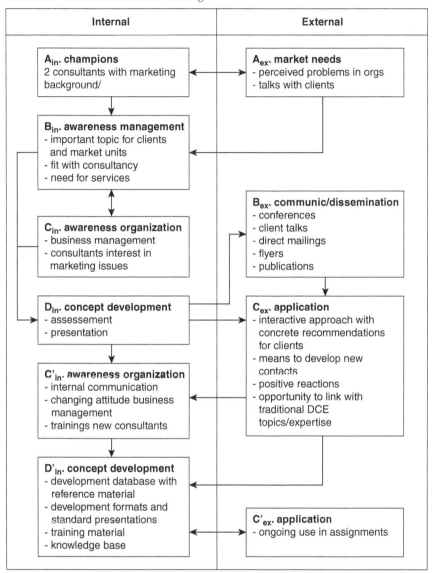

Awareness Management and Internal Organization

Both documents were discussed with the management of the consultancy. Initially, there were serious doubts about the fit of the new management idea with the existing DCE competencies and products. Until then, DCE concentrated particularly on IT, organizational, and process-related themes and had never been involved in marketing assignments for clients. However, these champions persuaded management to take the idea onto the list of service propositions. At the same time, the champions sought to create 'awareness' for the product-in-development within DCE by circulating the presentation among the various market-sector managers and discussing its relevance for their own sectors. The champions thus propagated the new idea in the organization and tried to find sponsors throughout the firm. Initially, these talks were cumbersome as the sector managers had little affinity and experience with marketing issues. The results of these efforts were therefore mixed. Some sector managers considered Marketing Excellence as a potential issue for their market sector, but most of them followed a 'wait-and-see' policy. Arrangements were made with the few interested sector managers about the introduction of Marketing Excellence within their sectors.

Some aspects were deemed crucial for the management idea's further development at that time. First, the champions made clear to top management of the consultancy that Marketing Excellence was considered a relevant, timely, and durable issue both by clients as well as some of the market units. Secondly, the top management became convinced that the idea would fit in the firm's portfolio of high-level services. Thirdly, the champions were able to persuade top management that the management idea would contribute to DCE's unique selling proposition of its market segments compared to competing consultancies.

Development and Application

Parallel to the talks with the business managers, a team of several consultants with interest and sympathy for marketing issues was formed and started with further developing the new management idea. The initial 'products' of this commodification process constituted an assessment model and an awareness presentation. This assessment model was considered a so-called growth or maturity tool in which a client organization is ranked according to a number of criteria in one of the five 'levels of excellence'. The key of the Marketing Excellence 'product' entails an elaborate questionnaire to assess the maturity level of the marketing organization. Furthermore, these are related to the organization's strategy. Thereby, three generic strategies are used as frame of reference. Finally, the client's marks on the different aspects are judged in light of the performance of other firms from the same sector in the Marketing Excellence benchmark database.

Because the assessment model had been worked out in detail, and much attention was given to the internal guidance of consultants and business managers, a number of consultants could be trained in applying the assessments in a relatively short period of time. Moreover, one of the champions was always present in talks with potential clients. This allowed him to bring in his knowledge and experience, while at the same time less experienced colleagues received 'on the job' training. The consultants involved considered the marketing assessment model an adequate instrument to generate new clients in the field of marketing. Its application entailed an interactive approach that generated a number of concrete recommendations for the client. After the assessment, a feedback session was organized to discuss the performance of the client organization. In this session, the clients' marketing activities were regarded in light of the business strategy and the performance related to competitors. On the basis of this, recommendations were given that were aimed at improving the clients' marketing organization, marketing strategy, marketing focus, and projects.

Projects were generally executed under the banner of Marketing Excellence. This label was used in all 'preassignment communication' with clients, such as documentation, initial talks, and the initial assessment. However, the term Marketing Excellence was considered to be of less importance than the terminology used within the client organization. Sometimes, 'local' terms were adopted while retaining Marketing Excellence's way of working. In addition, the terms-in-use were tailored to fit the sector-specific languages. For instance the use of English terms is more common in the Banking sector than in Public sector organizations and therefore specific marketing terms were adapted in the questionnaires that were used in health care agencies. At the same time there were no changes in the central principles of the new knowledge product. In this way it became possible to build up a database that was used for cross-comparative research.

The data generated in the talks with clients and particularly in the assessments were fed back to the development team. This was used to further develop formats and standardize client presentations. Also the Marketing Excellence projects generated reference material that was stored into a database. On this basis, the consultancy was able to enhance the knowledge 'product' as well as inform and instruct new consultants who were still unfamiliar with it. In a later phase, new elements were added to the initial 'product', resulting in a set of interrelated components including Marketing Balanced Scorecard, Marketing Process Atlas (in which the marketing activities from the assessment are described), the Marketing Excellence Improvement Program, and a Management Game that were placed under the banner of the management idea. In relation to these 'components' an elaborate internal training module has been developed to educate consultants to work with the new tools and improve their knowledge about marketing issues.

Internal and External Communication

The development team continuously paid significant attention to the internal communication about the management idea-in-development. More specifically, because the coordinator of the team kept an account of all client organizations and assessments, the DCE business managers continuously received information about the results of the new 'product'. Next to these reports, e-mails, and personal talks about the management idea, the development process has been discussed in the formal management meetings. The increasing number of assessments and the positive responses of the clients to this approach resulted in a gradual change in opinion of the sector managers towards the Marketing Excellence 'product'. Those who were initially hesitant about the new idea became enthusiastic as soon as its market success was becoming visible. It quickly became apparent that the assignments that followed the Marketing Excellence implementation for clients went beyond marketing issues. As a result, in the consultancy, Marketing Excellence 'product' was more and more considered as a lever for other businesses. These follow-up assignments for the clients entailed themes in which DCE was traditionally very strong such as change management, process streamlining, project management, interim management, and application selections. From this moment, the attention for and interest into this new management idea increased quickly throughout the consultancy also resulting in an enhanced legitimacy and related power position for the initial champions.

Not only internally, but also outside the consultancy firm information about the Marketing Excellence 'product' had been disseminated, for example via the DCE magazine that is published specifically for external relations. In addition, DCE organized two conferences about Marketing Excellence in collaboration with a university and several professional organizations in the field of marketing. These conferences constituted a platform to present the results of the assessments as well as to 'test' new ideas and developments about Marketing Excellence among the most important target group, the marketing managers in client organizations. Next to this conference, the topic was raised in the regular talks with clients. These were talks that emerged from the current network of DCE clients but also related to direct mail efforts. The mailing efforts were followed from the different market sectors. Also the 'product' Marketing Excellence and the related services were described on a flyer that was distributed on the market. Eventually, the term M-Xcellence was established as a trademark and is used in all commercial activities of the DCE consultants. Marketing Excellence was the initial working title but the trademark has gradually replaced this.

CONCLUSION

Drawing on a market orientation perspective, the present chapter constitutes a first step in exploring the initial stages in the life of a management idea. The case illustrates how market information, generated from a variety of different sources, is used internally to shape opinions and decisions of different groups of professionals in relation to the development of a new management idea. The design of the study provided important opportunities to reveal key elements in the way knowledge entrepreneurs shape the process of market sensing that have been hidden in the current research on the supply-side dynamics of management ideas. More specifically, this research allowed the generation of more insight into what market sensing means for the consultants involved in processes of knowledge commodification. By showing the importance of (1) continuously performing market information processing activities throughout the entire process and (2) internal organizational capabilities that enable learning about clients, this chapter opened up this black box and provided a more complex conceptualization of market sensing as a continuous interaction between internal and external dimensions, thereby shedding more light on how consultancies seek to keep their knowledge commodities in tune with market demand.

Thus first of all, this shows that market sensing is not regarded as a distinct or separate activity, but considered an integral element of every phase of the management knowledge commodification process. Moreover, the way this takes shape depends on the specific development stage. In early phases, market sensing is understood as generating information in talks with a small group of clients in a consultant's own network and involves more general information about the market needs. Later phases of market sensing are related to the information generated from the performance of assignments within client organizations and the reactions from larger scale communication events, which involve more specific and detailed ideas.

Second, this research also stresses the role of senior management and interdepartmental dynamics as key elements shaping the market sensing process of the management idea-in-development. Specifically, in the early phases, market information not only serves as an input for the commodification venture, but also is mainly used to internally legitimize new forms of expertise by convincing the consultancy's top management and the management of the different sector groups, and by creating awareness among peers. This may pave the way for a 'champion' to further develop a piece of expertise and commercialize it on the market. It is only during later phases that consultants use market information to shape the content of a new knowledge product in more detail, that is, particularly during its dissemination and application.

4   Structural Tensions

I have argued in the previous chapter that management ideas may not always exist in commodified forms, and showed how processes of market sensing may shape how these ideas move in and out of a 'commodity situation'. In particular, it is indicated that providing a useful consulting service requires more than referring to a best-selling book. As Huczynski (1993: 238) noted, a publication is only a starting point to create an audience and promote the author's name. Therefore consultants are likely involved in construction of an internal repertoire that will support the commercialization and implementation of a 'new' idea (Fincham and Evans, 1999; Huczynski, 1993; Morris, 2001; Visscher, 2001; Werr, 1999). However, as illustrated by the case discussion, to do this involves constantly moving between external and internal spheres.

I will now zoom in on the internal or 'backstage' dimensions to explore structural characteristics of management consultancies and their influence on processes and consequences of commodification. Indeed, given the low barriers of entry, the heterogeneity in consultants' background and the resultant 'bewildering range of services' (Clark and Fincham, 2002: 4) it can be expected that consultancies are not particularly uniform in the way in which the underlying repertoire is managed. Various studies have related the differences in consultancies' knowledge base to the structural characteristics of the firm, which become apparent in distinct 'business models' and related value propositions (Morris and Empson, 1998; Hansen et al., 1999). For instance Visscher (2001) pointed out that in a centralized, technique-oriented strategy, a consultancy builds a coherent arrangement of well-elaborated techniques around a leading model. In contrast, deploying a more diversified, prudence-oriented strategy implies that a consultancy builds up a collection of different, loosely coupled, and multipurpose tools that enhance flexibility and support the handling of a range of organizational problems.

Therefore this chapter will draw on innovation literature to explore similarities and differences in the structural routes through which new commodified forms of knowledge are developed within consultancies as well as the unavoidable managerial tension that this may engender. The innovation literature suggests that such a development process involves moving through specific activities and inevitably generates managerial tensions. In the following section, I discuss the innovation literature and identify a number of key activities with respect to new development ventures, as well as the managerial tensions that accompany this process. Next, I empirically explore typical forms of knowledge commodification processes within consultancies and highlight the specific managerial problems associated with them. In a concluding section, I discuss our findings in relation to the literature on management knowledge commodification and the production of management ideas.

AN INNOVATION PERSPECTIVE

Key Activities

A continuous need for new management knowledge commodities frequently impels consultancies to renew their repertoire in support of their services. Drawing on extensive innovation research, I show in the following section that developing new products generally requires a number of key activities: (1) initiation; (2) formation; and (3) realization, involving both (a) construction, and (b) dissemination. While these are perhaps not exhaustive, they do highlight a number of crucial elements in the innovation process. After describing these activities, I suggest that innovation efforts inevitably generate managerial problems induced by the organizational tensions inherent in performing these activities.

Although product development processes in organizations may follow many different trajectories (Cooper, 1983), the innovation literature suggests that these efforts share some common activities. A first constellation of activities concentrates on the deliberate initiation of innovative efforts by organizational actors. Innovation theorists emphasize that organizations habitually focus on exploiting existing operations (Burns and Stalker, 1961; Dougherty and Hardy, 1996). As Burns and Stalker (1961: 21) stated, introducing novelty in any organization is not without risk. New development initiatives do not generally emerge automatically, but involve generating attention for still unrealized ideas and persuading people to invest in developing these ideas (see also van de Ven, 1986). Here, various theorists have distinguished between an emphasis on strategic planning versus emerging entrepreneurship (Burgelman, 1983; Twiss, 1992). Innovation efforts may be derived from a process of strategic planning in which ideas are focused, and where a strategic choice is made as to which options to respond to. This may result in formal project definitions that describe the objectives and trajectory needed to realize a new product (Wheelwright and Clark, 1992). However, much of the work does not lend itself to detailed planning, and this allows development initiatives to emerge as a spontaneous outcome of individual efforts in organizations (Benghozi, 1990).

A second central activity in a development process concerns the formation of different groups of people and resources involved in a new product development effort. The innovation literature suggests that the demand that innovative activities place on these groups and resources cannot easily be reconciled with the claims of routine organization, and that innovation thus inevitably raises conflicting situations in organizations (Vermeulen, 2001: 154). Clark and Fujimoto (1991: 255) demonstrated that organizations may deploy a heavyweight project manager structure that has a strong influence across different functions, and which carries a formal responsibility for product development. Other studies have shown that innovative efforts may assume a more informal basis that allows flexibility and enables an idea to be led through the formal organization, avoiding obstructing standards and procedures (Benghozi, 1990; Schoonhoven and Jelinek, 1997). Here, a formation process becomes more dependent on the enthusiasm of individual people and their particular networks and experiences. In both instances, a 'soul of fire' (Stjernberg and Philips, 1993) or 'innovation champion' (Chakrabarti, 1974; Rogers, 1995: 398) is regarded as a vital factor in conveying enthusiasm and in attracting different groups to an innovative idea.

A third cluster of activities recognized by innovation theorists entails the actual 'realization' of an innovation. This involves (a) the 'construction' of ideas into concrete and commercially viable products or services. Such an activity is often represented as moving through a predetermined development trajectory, in which a set of functional demands are concretized through a series of integrated problem-solving cycles in making a concept outline, creating a detailed design, and testing a prototype (Clark and Fujimoto, 1991; Cooper, 1983; Tidd et al., 1997). Other researchers, however, describe a more experiential approach in which the construction of a product or service is closely connected to its application in the market (Moorman and Miner, 1998).

Innovation is not solely about constructing a product or service; it also involves (b) its 'dissemination' throughout the organization. This aspect has received little attention in the new product development literature. However, innovation has been defined in terms of 'the development and implementation of new ideas' (van de Ven, 1986: 390), suggesting that a new idea has to be institutionalized and incorporated into the practices of the innovating organization. Specifically, this involves managing the introduction in such a way that different organizational members across an organization accept an idea, and that they are able to manufacture and commercialize it (Jelinek and Schoonhoven, 1990: 337). Innovation theorists argue that convincing people of an innovation's 'relative advantage' (Rogers, 1995) involves a sociopolitical process that necessitates a continuous regeneration of legitimacy (Stjernberg and Phillips, 1993; van de Ven, 1986). This often creates a dilemma between facilitating a process of local learning and discovery versus deploying a more top-down approach to diffusion.

Insoluble Tensions

Accounts of new product development emphasize the persistence of managerial problems inherent in specific development activities (Dougherty, 1996). Such problems continuously crystallize in a persistent tension between freedom and control. Twiss (1992: 37) explained this tension in terms of the need for control of expensive activities while providing an organizational environment open to the generation and development of new ideas. This suggests that organizational receptiveness to novelty benefits from an environment in which the initiatives of devoted individuals can be developed without the constraints of tight regulation. However, a well-defined formal structure and a degree of bureaucracy are necessary to ensure corporate control over development projects. This tension has been the subject of long-standing debates on the interplay between loose and tight management systems (Benghozi, 1990; Burns and Stalker, 1961; Dougherty, 1996; Jelinek and Schoonhoven, 1990; Lewis et al., 2002; Moorman and Miner, 1998), suggesting that dealing with specific organizational tensions emerging from new product development activities requires an ability to combine both a disciplined and a loose approach.

This brief review suggests that activities and problems with new product development have been recognized for a long time in the literature on product innovation. Our intention in the next part of the chapter is to explore how these activities and tensions take shape within consultancies involved in the development of new management knowledge commodities.

FORMS OF KNOWLEDGE COMMODIFICATION

Conflicting Demands

In this section, I show that new knowledge commodification ventures in consultancies may become an important basis for tensions. This means that managing development efforts involves dealing with the conflicting demands of freedom and control. As one consultant expressed it, 'In a consultancy one will always find a tension between efficiency and the need for freedom of individual consultants' (C2). On the one hand, consultancy work is often associated with a degree of professional autonomy, and consultants feel impelled to develop their own vision and approach to a new commodity. Here one consultant noted:

> Actually, you want to develop a concept by yourself because that is the crown of it all. (P3)

While another stated:

> Generally, a consultant always wants to put his personal mark on a concept, because that is highly related to his ego. (T2)

Promoting successful commodified forms of management knowledge also provides an opportunity to become respected as an expert in the field and can be beneficial to a consultant's career. The lack of a material component in ideas allows consultants to develop their own specific repertoire underlying a management idea. As one consultant who developed a BPR approach argued:

> I just made a mixture of a number of books I had read, my own experiences, my vision on organizations, my experiences in consultancy, Hammer and Champy, a book of Arthur Andersen, and we used a large number of ideas from Sociotechnical Systems Design for process design. (N2)

Hence, the interpretative space of management ideas easily invites consultants to translate a management idea in their own specific way that satisfies a need for professional autonomy. On the other hand, a consultancy firm may benefit from the deployment of a more disciplined approach that controls development efforts. Such an approach may provide a company-wide focus for the selection and resourcing of ideas-in-development. This may enable the introduction of a single clear-cut innovation in the market, and mean that the wheel is not invented and reinvented at different places within a consultancy.

> With such a common focus, you can control the entire organization because you decide at a central level which things you will take up, and by this you can tell more easily a clear story to the client. (C2)

At the same time, a disciplined approach may constrain the interpretative space of a management idea. Such homogenization contributes to a degree of coherence in the development and application of an underlying repertoire:

> Obviously you have to determine the nomenclature and vocabulary for the organization. It is rather clumsy if people in England talk about it in a different way than people in the Netherlands. (F2)

Such a tension potentially means a consultancy constantly feels the need to choose between professional and corporate forms of management knowledge commodification. The first typical form is mainly driven by the professional interests and by initiatives of individual consultants. In the second form, development ventures are primarily driven by corporate efforts. The following section elaborates and illustrates these different typical forms with respect to the central activities in the development process: (1) initiation, (2) formation, and (3) realization involving both construction and dissemination (see Table 4.1).

Table 4.1 Forms of management knowledge commodification

Development activities	Corporate-driven form	Professional-driven form
Initiation	Local interests and initiatives of individual consultants	Strategic decision of top management
Formation	Clustering of consultants around specific types of assignments	Appointment and support of project group independent from direct assignments
Construction	Gradual development of repertoire, particularly fed by new assignments	Development of complete repertoire particularly fed by a company's best practices
Dissemination	Gradual extension of network of peers and clients	Organization-wide distribution

Professional-driven Form

The 'initiation' of knowledge commodification in a professional-driven form can be characterized by the continuous emergence of local development ventures, each driven by the efforts of one or several consultants. Whether an idea will be taken up and developed into an elaborate repertoire largely depends on the initiative of the individual consultant(s). 'The most important reason to take up that concept lay particularly in the intrinsic drive of a few people who just liked it' (U1). Or, as another consultant put it:

> If there is someone who likes to do it, he will just do it. Concerning this, I think the strategy is rather emerging here. (E1)

This form of commodification requires the enthusiasm and entrepreneurship of several consultants who strongly believe in the business opportunities of a knowledge 'product', and who are able to transmit this initial enthusiasm to their colleagues and clients. This interest often lies dormant in 'professional hobbies'; but when these hobbies yield income, development activities are likely to start up. The 'formation' of resources around such initiatives is not specifically induced by top management, but resembles an organic process driven by the interests and experiences of consultants and fueled by their interactions with clients. Here, informal networks may cluster around joint projects with clients and create platforms of exchange of professional experiences.

> There was clearly no formal project group set up with the idea to just develop our BPR approach. (W2)

This form requires consulting firms having a relatively weak departmental structure and a pool of relatively autonomous people that gather around temporarily prominent ideas and practices.

> At the moment, it appears that a professional hobby has certain opportunities in the market. Consultants will develop things together, because you are not able to do everything on your own. (P3)

This makes the individual ability to obtain assignments and resources for commodification ventures crucial.

> Often within a consulting organization a concept champion emerges. And it depends on his formal position, his charisma, the extent this person is able to inspire other consultants, and his commercial successes whether a concept may expand in a consulting firm. (K3)

So, an innovation champion not only has to believe in an idea, but also needs to attract clients and assemble an internal network of disciples. The 'construction' of a repertoire is characterized by an incremental process that is shaped in relatively close relationship to a consultancy's assignments. Here, consulting projects become the most important vehicle for commodification ventures.

> The creation of an elaborate proposition for that client compelled us to write out a methodology. (W2)

These project experiences were used to codify clusters of problem-solving approaches. Management knowledge commodification was thus closely related to its application and resulted in the continuous adaptation of a repertoire.

> At a new assignment, we just combined the knowledge of the preceding assignments. (V2)

So, the accumulation of knowledge about a management idea remains close to the consulting 'shop floor,' because it is strongly related to the projects a consultant is able to obtain and the strength of network ties with colleagues. In this form, the 'dissemination' of a repertoire in a consultancy involves enlarging a network of clients and colleague consultants who become concerned with a knowledge commodification venture. This may lead to locally initiated internal marketing efforts to inform and enthuse other consultants about a management idea-in-development. Specifically, consultants may provide small-scale internal training sessions and explain the business opportunities of the new 'product'. An important element in the increased receptiveness of other consultants is the commercial success of a commodification venture, as one consultant observed:

As a small working group, we are busy elaborating the concept, and herewith try to find more enthusiastic people within the firm. [. . .] Owing to the success of the method, people become enthusiastic and it increasingly generates attention. (B2)

This implies that dissemination is characterized by forms of evangelism to enlarge the professional network of consultants involved in a specific management knowledge commodification venture.

Corporate-driven Form

In a corporate-driven form, knowledge commodification is 'initiated' by a consultancy's senior management. The initiation of a new commodification venture remains reserved to a central unit:

In this organization these things generally occur in a centralized way. So it was also a central initiative from the headquarters in . . . that we had to become involved in BPR. (F2)

Here, the decision to take up a management idea is preceded by a corporate selection process within which market signals are mapped and promising ideas are drawn through a development funnel (Wheelwright and Clark, 1992).

The people within this level decide about the new themes and new ideas within this firm, and everything in the domain of research is directed by it. (Q1)

Eventually, a firm focuses on a selected number of ideas by allocating resources to the most promising development activities. In this form, a management knowledge commodification venture becomes regarded as a corporate investment in which the company's expertise is concentrated. Initiating a knowledge commodification effort becomes a deliberate strategy of a consultancy to systematically stimulate the exploration of a company-wide repertoire. The 'formation' of resources around corporate development initiatives involves the creation and facilitation of a central working team consisting of leading experts within the organization. The establishment of such a development venture requires a consultancy to allocate funds.

Central management made a budget available for the development of the BPR method because it had become a hot issue in the market. (P4)

Generally, this form of knowledge commodification is associated with substantial corporate ex ante expenditures without a direct link to present client projects. So when it is decided to allocate resources to specific development activities

> . . . an assignment was given from the central division to build a team. (F2)

Team members are selected on the basis of their experiences and competencies, and are drawn away from their consulting assignments. This group is provided with a clear-cut task and is facilitated from a central level to develop a complete and coherent repertoire available to the entire consulting organization. The 'construction' of a consulting repertoire underlying a new management idea is not an incremental process, but involves the development of a full framework before its market launch. Such a framework is topped up with best practices that are not developed from scratch, but different 'goodies' are derived from knowledge items across the entire organization.

> We compared all existing methods within [consulting firm P] and eventually worked out a number of phases. (P4)

This type of construction process remains relatively independent of assignments related to a consulting 'product', but involves assembling a complete solution in advance in such a way that consultants are able to apply it instantly:

> The BPR method is turned into a half-product in which, for each phase, the aspects you had to deal with were indicated. Within each phase a number of deliverables had to be realized if one wants to make any progress to a change process in a justified way. (P4)

Finally, the 'dissemination' of a management idea's underlying repertoire within a consulting firm is strongly associated with large-scale distribution efforts by means of manuals, intranet-based information systems, and obligatory training curricula. One consultant noted that this dissemination effort

> . . . showed itself in large manuals and courses in the large education center in which you were drilled, after which you were considered to roll it out in your own country. (X1)

This form not only involves the large-scale distribution of a repertoire, but also the pressure actually to use it.

> We present the [consulting firm T] method to our consultants and state that they may use it or develop their own method, only we clearly emphasize that the latter is particularly clumsy. (T2)

INTRODUCING NOVELTY AND TENSIONS

A Supply of Problems

Consultancies are caught between contrasting forms of management knowledge commodification that cannot easily be reconciled. Our data illustrate that each form of commodification cannot be applied without further complications. In particular, deploying these forms separately is associated with significant managerial problems, but the coexistence of both typical forms within one consultancy is also hypothesized to give rise to significant frictions.

First, a professional-driven form takes the 'professional hobbies' of individual consultants as a starting point, and commodification efforts are characterized by an incremental trajectory in which a repertoire is shaped and fed by the assignments a consultant is able to obtain. This means that knowledge commodification is highly dependent on the more-or-less coincidental interest of individuals and their ability to create a network of enthusiastic clients and colleague consultants. As a result, the risk that consultancies may 'miss the boat' is much higher both in the adoption, as well as in the entrenchment, of knowledge associated with a 'product'. Moreover, this form of commodification allows for the possibility that similar 'products' crop up at different places within one consultancy. Due to the relative autonomy of a heterogeneous group of professionals and the interpretative space of a management idea, it can become 'translated' in different ways. As a result, 'different clones' (T1) of the same knowledge 'product' can emerge within a consultancy. This is not considered useful either in the market approach or the internal sharing of knowledge:

> Within [consulting firm P] a situation emerged in which we had five different BPR approaches. We only found that out at the moment we provided different offers at one client. (P2)

Specifically, in a professional-driven form, consultants desire a degree of freedom for their interpretations and the autonomy to develop their own repertoire. This means that these professionals are not inclined simply to 'adopt' another set of methods and tools.

> . . . of course everyone had invested in their own approach and were not willing to simply throw these overboard. (P2)

However, addressing these inadequacies by adopting a corporate-driven form may induce considerable frictions; as a result, such corporate efforts may encounter significant dissemination problems. Whereas the professional form allows consultants largely to decide for themselves whether a management idea fits their mindset or whether they can do something with it, the corporate form means that consultants may search far less easily for alternatives when they are forced to deploy a specific repertoire.

> If you force consultants too much into a standardized framework driven by the taste of the market by sending them to a CRM course, and let them tell clients to implement CRM, a number of people will leave [. . .]. (C2)

We have seen that the corporate-driven form may be associated with risk reduction, in the sense that in the development of new knowledge commodities little is left to chance. Here, only a few promising ideas are initiated and receive corporate support. This allows particular consultancies to present a unitary approach to the market, which distinguishes them from consultancies that are not able to make these large investments. Moreover the risk decreases that the wheel is being reinvented at several places within a consultancy. At the same time, such a form involves a significantly higher degree of risk for the consultancy as a whole, compared to a more organic form, since it is paralleled with significant capital-intensive development investments. This means that when the popularity of a 'product' turns out to be disappointing, it has immediate consequences for the entire consultancy. This form of management knowledge commodification not only runs considerable risks for the consulting company as a whole, but may also absorb the energy of development initiatives of individual consultants.

> One should not destroy the energy inherent in the people by dictating something from a central level. (P3)

The continuous initiation of large-scale initiatives makes knowledge commodification easily regarded as an institution in itself. Turning a repertoire underlying a saleable 'product' into a dictum will inevitably frustrate the development efforts of individual consultants. However, dealing with these problems by deploying a professional driven form next to an institutionalized corporate form may result in significant controversies. In consulting firms deploying a strong corporate-driven form, individual consultants are not expected to spend their time on development activities. One consultant observed that, in his organization:

> Much is centralized and people are not expected to develop things themselves. (X1)

This tends to mean that there are few incentives for initiating such development efforts within a consultancy, because novel commodities are worked out at a central level and generating income is the dominant criterion, instead of generating novel ideas. Individual-driven commodification initiatives are quickly obstructed in a corporate form-dominated consultancy.

At a certain moment, I was very frustrated in doing development activities and research. (X1)

Compensating Mechanisms

As argued in the previous section, consultancies have to choose between opposed forms of management knowledge commodification. Both forms have significant drawbacks and cause serious frictions when they coexist in a consultancy. In this section, I argue that consultancies are not likely to solve the problems associated with knowledge commodification themselves, but can only deploy mechanisms that tend to minimize the shortcomings of each typical form in different ways (see Table 4.2). First, a consultancy may transform local practices into corporate efforts. Here, early commodification activities remain dependent upon the initiatives and out-of-pocket expenditures of individual consultants.

> Partly, you allow hobbies to exist because they generate energy for the people, but at the same time you monitor what they yield for the organization. (P3)

When a consultancy firm discovers that some are becoming successful in the market, these professional-driven ventures are quickly turned into a corporate development activity.

> If it eventually turns out to be a success, you will get all the support you can get, because you may do anything if it generates income. (P3)

The initiating person may claim time and resources to develop a particular repertoire and manage it in a more disciplined way. Granting time to

Table 4.2 Structural problems and compensating mechanisms

	Professional-driven form		Corporate-driven form	
Key problems	Development of focus		Development of entrepreneurship	
Compensating mechanisms	Expand successful local practices	Support selected local ideas-in-development	Reinforce interaction of local idea generation and decisions for further development	Stimulate interpretative space for translation of abstract repertoire to concrete client-situations

develop a repertoire allows consultants to construct an enhanced market approach and gives more continuity to the knowledge associated with it. Thus, by accounting for the conservation of professional energy, a consultancy may influence the process of management knowledge commodification.

Second, a consultancy may provide funding for only a selected number of consultants who seek to develop new commodified forms of knowledge. In contrast with the previous mechanism, these ideas will not have been elaborated when the decision is made to support a local initiative from the corporate level.

> At [consulting firm C], we have the 'Fundatie,' which donates money to consultants within [firm C] to do research, so that you can come out with something more robust. (C2)

This requires consultancies holding a budget for development activities and, by submitting a proposal for a new 'product', individual consultants have the opportunity to be considered for funding.

> You have to write a plan and, on the basis of that plan, it is decided whether you are granted a certain amount of money. (C2)

In this way, the initiatives for development activities may come from individual consultants, while decisions for funding are still taken on a more central level. This allows consultants to reserve time for fundamental development activities without being dependent on the availability of projects in a certain area. The likely result is a repertoire that can be introduced in the consultancy and in the market, after which practice decides whether it is applicable.

Third, a consultancy may stimulate a highly structured company-wide iteration between locally generated market signals, on the one hand, and corporate decisions about which themes are turned into development activities, on the other. Unlike previous mechanisms, here the process of idea generation is decoupled from the process of commodification.

> We seek to invite everybody in this firm to generate all kinds of ideas and put them on the radar screen. (Q1)

So in this case every consultant in a firm can produce ideas, but that does not mean they are allowed to work on them. On a corporate level, it is decided which ideas are interesting for the consultancy and to what extent resources are allocated to specific development activities.

> We put our own project teams on the most promising ideas that emerge from it. (Q1)

From a central level, people are selected to participate in teams responsible for a particular commodification venture. Finally, when the entire process of commodification involving initiation, formation, and realization is located at the corporate level, a consultancy may deploy a dissemination strategy that seeks to appeal to professional values. However, the internal dissemination of an elaborated repertoire within a consultancy can be very difficult, because consultants habitually relate uptake and application to their own professional interests. As a partner in a large consultancy argued:

> When consultants hear that they have to use it maybe a few will comply, but most of them rather not. (T2)

Here, consultancies can deploy a mechanism that allows consultants partly to develop their own version of a consultancy 'product' when it is shaped to the specific client's needs. This means that a consultancy limits and controls the interpretative space of a management idea by providing an elaborate repertoire, but at the same time seeks to appeal to professional values by stressing the possibilities for interpretation, giving consultants the feeling that it is partly their own work.

> If they take up the corporate approach, we indicate that they can shape it in their own way at an assignment, because every client is different. (T2)

As a result, it is not regarded as a wholly corporate repertoire because it also includes a consultant's own input.

CONCLUSION

In this chapter I used the innovation literature as a starting point to empirically explore forms of management knowledge commodification in consultancies, and to explain how these firms deal with the significant problems associated with it. This brought us to a deeper understanding of the structural conditions that shape the way processes in relation to management knowledge commodification take shape in consultancies.

First, this analysis showed that supplying management ideas involves much more than simply adopting fashionable rhetoric and promoting it on public display. Rather, as with any organization that seeks to renew its services, turning a new management idea into a useful repertoire is associated with proceeding through a particular development process within a consultancy. The chapter suggests that a first constellation of activities is related to the initiation of innovative ventures by consultants. A second central activity in a development process concerns the formation of a group of capable people including the generation of resources. A final cluster of activities that is identified entails the construction of a repertoire to support the commercialization and implementation of a management idea and the dissemination of this repertoire throughout the consultancy.

Second, while these ventures may share some general activities, the development trajectories display important differences. In this chapter I demonstrated that the way these commodification activities are carried out varies considerably and may diverge between professional-driven and corporate-driven forms. One typical development form identified in this chapter is mainly driven by the professional interests and initiatives of individual consultants and fuelled by their interactions with clients. The initiation of this form can be characterized by the continuous emergence of local development ventures, each driven by the efforts of one or several consultants. Here commodification efforts are characterized primarily by an incremental trajectory in which a repertoire is shaped and fed by the assignments a consultant is able to obtain. In another typical form, commodification is mainly driven by corporate efforts to systematically facilitate the exploration of a complete repertoire that is disseminated throughout the entire consultancy. Here only a few promising ideas are initiated and receive corporate support. This form is characterized by the explicit involvement of a firm's top management.

Third, the discussion in this chapter demonstrates that the activities involved in developing commodified forms of management knowledge bring significant organizational problems. In particular, consultancies are confronted by a tension between the corporate need for a disciplined development approach, and a need for the professional autonomy of individual consultants, elements that cannot be easily reconciled. Although these problems cannot be solved, consultancies demonstrated various mechanisms to minimize the shortcomings. For instance consultancies may seek to enhance focus in their commodification ventures by (1) transforming successful local practices into corporate efforts or (2) providing funding for only a selected number of consultants who submit plans for developing new forms of commodified knowledge. This allows consultants to reserve time for commodification activities without being dependent on the availability of client projects in a certain area. In addition, to enhance entrepreneurship among their present staff of consultants consultancies may (1) follow a highly structured company-wide iteration system between locally generated market signals, and corporate decisions about which themes are turned into development activities or (2) deploy a system that allows consultants to participate in the process of commodification when adapting the repertoire to the specific client's or sector needs.

5 Gaining Currency

The previous chapter zoomed in on relevant internal dimensions to explore structural characteristics of management consultancies and their influence on processes and consequences of commodification. The present chapter builds on this by providing an understanding of the process in which management ideas gain 'good currency' within the system of knowledge supply. As indicated in the introductory chapter, the 'social life' of a management idea tends to be reified for various reasons, not the least because of the interests of knowledge entrepreneurs to enhance the exchange value of their 'products'. As a result, the process of knowledge commodification is often considered linear and unproblematic, merely concerned with jointly transforming new ideas into marketable commodities. In this, the development of successful commodities is habitually presented as a series of logical and straightforward phases unavoidably resulting in a product that can be immediately sold on the market for management solutions. In addition, it is argued that when ideas are formed and processed to meet clients' needs this is immediately supported by various collaborative relationships at the 'backstage'. This suggests that commodification constitutes a harmonious process that automatically enjoys the assistance of many other people within knowledge entrepreneurs.

However, as I argue in the later sections, this conceptualization is significantly at odds with the view presented by the new product development literature. This shows that product innovation does not involve merely moving through a series of logical phases or does not particularly generate collaborative relations within the production system. Rather, the development of new ideas in organizations is often highly contested and generally encounters substantial resistance (Burns and Stalker, 1961; Dougherty and Hardy, 1996; Jones and Stevens, 1999; Vermeulen, 2001). Therefore, it requires substantial internal effort to turn an idea into a successful commodity and convince others of its market value. The research in this chapter explores the possibility of viewing commodification as a contested process within knowledge suppliers. I focus on the internal establishment process of new knowledge products. It starts from the viewpoint that commodities that are now regarded as successful on the market were not necessarily so self-evident at the time they were produced. Using interviews with management consultants, the study provides an understanding of the internal elements that may encourage or inhibit the commodification process. The chapter identifies major bases for impediments to linking new knowledge products with the organization, thereby emphasizing the importance of internal legitimation efforts. This shows the significance of considering and further studying the sociopolitical process in which new management ideas gain 'good currency' (van de Ven, 1986) within knowledge entrepreneurs.

In the next section I discuss the current literature on product innovation and legitimacy because it offers an understanding of the persistent problems in developing a new management idea into a marketable product. Specifically, I discuss some central impediments to the establishment of new ideas and stress the importance of gaining currency. Subsequently, I show how management consultants perceive important bases for intraorganizational struggles that unavoidably accompany this processes knowledge commodification in praxis. The chapter concludes with implications for the conceptualization of knowledge commodification and the literature on management ideas.

COMMODIFICATION AS NEW PRODUCT DEVELOPMENT

Impediments to Product Development

Innovation theorists explain the difficulties and ambiguities associated with new product development from the conflicting claims or 'tensions' inherent in performing these activities (Dougherty, 1996; Schoonhoven and Jelinek, 1997). The new product development literature shows that conflicting interests and priorities in organizations become particularly apparent in reconciling innovative activities with an organization that is mainly designed to maintain existing practices. Established organizational routines are often unable to accommodate innovative activities, systematically causing notable difficulties in dealing with the uncertainties and changes associated with developing new ideas. As Burns and Stalker (1961) noted, the strength of the political system and current 'status structure' tend to confirm the status quo within an organization. Such elements cause important barriers, thereby persistently obstructing the realization of new ideas.

To further understand the persistence of difficulties with product innovation, Dougherty and Heller (1994) draw on an institutional approach. Their study shows that key activities related to developing new products generally do not fit into the habitualized patterns of thought and action in various ways. The realization of new ideas may violate existing organizational practices or may be 'unthinkable' in the light of the institutionalized thought structure. Therefore, activities to develop new products are easily considered 'illegitimate' (Dougherty and Heller, 1994) within organizations. This becomes apparent as a lack of understanding, but also in resistance to the development of new ideas. As a result, connecting new products to the organization's strategy and resources—a linking mechanism essential to the appreciation and realization of new products—is easily obstructed (Burgelman, 1983; Burns and Stalker, 1961; Dougherty and Hardy, 1996; Jones and Stevens, 1999).

Therefore, developing commercially successful innovations is not restricted to simply making a new idea into a product, but involves managing the establishment of a new product within the organization (Clark and Fujimoto, 1991; Cooper, 1983; Tidd et al., 1997; Twiss, 1992). As van de Ven states, a new idea can only be regarded as an innovation when it is institutionalized and thereby 'incorporated in the taken for granted assumptions and thought structure of organizational practice' (1986: 604). This indicates that it is essential to regard product innovation as a collective activity in which novelty has to become interwoven into established thoughts and actions (Berger and Luckmann, 1966; Hargadon and Douglas, 2001; Tolbert and Zucker, 1996; van de Ven, 1986). However, as argued previously, this process is often problematic because of inertial forces within organizations that cause major impediments to linking and collaboration.

Gaining Legitimacy

To overcome problems of linking product innovations with the organization's strategy and resources, Dougherty and Heller (1994) stressed the key role of legitimation activities, and showed various ways in which innovators seek to explain and justify (Berger and Luckmann, 1966) novelty as valid organizational practice. Gaining legitimacy involves 'winning acceptance' (Suchman, 1995) for the innovative idea and for the people propagating it. This means that pioneers have to trigger people to pay attention to new ideas and persuade organizational members of the advantage of the new ideas over current practices (van de Ven, 1986). Gaining organizational support and resources for new ideas involves drawing on persuasive communication activities to make a favorable impression, thereby conveying the perception that a new idea can be converted into a commercially successful product (Brunsson, 1982; Prasad and Rubenstein, 1994; Tolbert and Zucker, 1996). Convincing others to support novelty involves considering two interrelated elements.

First, it is argued that several characteristics of the product innovation itself increase the possibility of the product becoming accepted as legitimate (Rogers, 1995; Twiss, 1992). A central element here is a new product's fit within the firm's existing business and measures. This includes being in tune with established strategic, marketing, financial, and production criteria (Twiss, 1992). This shows that although innovation implies novelty, its formal appreciation often requires compatibility and familiarity with existing standards and practices (Hargadon and Douglas, 2001; Rogers, 1995). Being associated with existing organizational routines and established procedures enhances legitimacy (Brown and Ennew, 1995; Tidd et al., 1997;

Twiss, 1992) and increases the likelihood that product innovations will acquire resources and become established within an organization.

Second, theorists have also emphasized that legitimization draws heavily on human agency. Novelty seeks to change the measures by which practices are perceived (Ortmann, 1995), and therefore it is crucial that people are able to understand and enact it. Information about the value of a new idea may be selectively interpreted and often does not lead to action (Cooper and Kleinschmidt, 1986; Deshpande and Zaltman, 1982). In other words, it is not enough for the realization of a new product to be presented in an attractive form; it also requires a change in existing power structures and established patterns of social activity (Dougherty and Heller, 1994). A key element in gaining legitimacy is a product champion (Chakrabarti, 1974; Clark and Fujimoto, 1991) or 'soul of fire' (Stjernberg and Philips, 1993) who has an interest and involvement in a new product's realization and is able to sell it to the decision makers in the organization. In addition, Chakrabarti (1974) argues that it is essential for a product champion to have political skills to overcome resistance and limit controversies during the realization of a new idea.

The following section illustrates the main themes by explaining consultants' understanding of how problems in commodification take shape. Although perhaps not exhaustive, I believe that it highlights some important bases that impede or enhance knowledge commodification, specifically with reference to a new idea's establishment within a knowledge supplier. The opinions of the consultants support our argument that knowledge commodification is regarded as a contested process within key suppliers of management knowledge. It is important to understand that the success of a commodity cannot be determined beforehand and therefore consultants have to internally legitimize new ideas. This indicates that, unlike what has been suggested by current conceptualizations of commodification, the internal collaboration within consultancies in the supply of management knowledge is not so self-evident.

STRUGGLES IN COMMODIFICATION

The analysis revealed that knowledge suppliers see commodification as a problematic effort. It shows that development efforts do not necessarily meet with a favorable response within consultancies and therefore are not widely supported or automatically generate collaborative initiatives. The consultants' comments made clear that a key problem lies in the (in)ability of linking these development efforts to the organization (see Table 5.1). The subsequent struggles become apparent in (1) internal criticism and disbelief about the value of a new idea and, that, in relation to this, shape (2) obstructions in the realization of a product-in-development. It is therefore that consultants see internal legitimation as a crucial base to increase (3) the likelihood of a commodity's establishment.

Table 5.1   Bases to struggles in commodification

Bases	Elements	Effects
Lack of perceived fit with existing business	• Incompatibility with existing practices • Inconsistency with firms image • Cannibalization • Violation of professional territory	Criticism and disbelief
Lack of involvement	• Inadequate support from management • Inadequate collaboration of individuals and departments	Obstructed implementation

Criticism and Disbelief

In this section I identify several important bases related to the product inno-vation itself that may increase criticism and disbelief within a consultancy. These bases likely inhibit the likelihood of being accepted as legitimate management knowledge 'product' in a consultancy. A key element in this is the new idea's perceived fit with the overall business of a consultancy. Al-though product innovation implies novelty, its company-wide appreciation requires compatibility and familiarity with existing standards and practices (Hargadon and Douglas, 2001; Rogers, 1995). A new product's incompat-ibility with the current product range of a consultancy is considered highly problematic, and a major reason for criticism, irrespective of the product's intrinsic merits. This means that within a management consultancy, estab-lished and institutionalized consulting practices may constitute considerable barriers to the emergence and development of new knowledge commodi-ties. In particular, the likelihood of conflict emerges when the prescriptions offered by a new 'product' are significantly at odds with existing ideas and established consulting practices:

> From the 1990s onwards much time and energy has been devoted to the development of the new concept within [consulting firm]. [. . .] In-ternally we had major discussions about the method because within [consulting firm K] there was also tough opposition. One of the charac-teristics of the method was that we let employees specify their ways of working themselves, but one of my colleagues within [consulting firm] was convinced that employees were not able to do that. [. . .] Next to this, he considered it to be detrimental to his own professional oc-cupation. About this subject angry letters have been published in the [consulting firm] internal magazine and a large polemic has developed around it. (K3)

Another potential barrier in the appreciation of new management ideas is constituted by the perceived inconsistency between a new 'product-in-development' and a firm's image. Building an image as a prominent expert in a specific field is essential given the difficulties of evaluating consultancy services (Alvesson, 1993; Clark, 1995). This makes it likely that the introduction of a new knowledge product that counters the established image of a firm offers a source of internal friction. Therefore, it may not be uncontroversial to be involved in commodification ventures when other consultants believe it does not fit the current image of their consultancy:

> Daring to say that you did not simply want to polish in TQM terms but seriously wanted to cut in organizations was rather new. In no way did consultants find that suitable for [consulting firm]. So internally it was not uncontroversial to do BPR-like assignments. [. . .] Within such a firm you always have a number of culture carriers, the semi-gurus, and they spoke with disdain about BPR and the group of cowboys propagating it. We therefore had to fight for our position in the consultancy. (W2)

At the same time, consultants emphasized the significance of considering the effects upon a company's wider portfolio of products if new management ideas were to be accepted. A danger of neglecting the current product range increases a possibility of cannibalization. The launch of a newly developed 'product' may directly affect demand for services in other parts of the organization. In particular, it can easily distract existing clients from current assignments. As a result, a new management idea may easily gain sales volume at the expense of established products. Within a consultancy this may lead to internal struggles with consultants exploiting current management ideas:

> Of course you want to enter the market with your new concepts and then you get an ordinary clash of interests from a specific unit of consultants that already had contacts with a specific client and then we come with new ideas at the same bank. The question is to what extent there is a matter of cannibalism and who is getting the money from where. [. . .] Although internally people may be very angry with me, I am still going to talk with that client. (Q1)

An important base for internal criticism is when development efforts are perceived by consultants as violating an established practice area or the territory of a specific group within a consultancy. Not surprisingly, this may result in substantial friction because the newcomers can easily take advantage of the initial investments in expertise and reputation of pioneering consultants:

> Within my area, nobody got the space to do development activities because I was the man. Everything just had to be linked up with my

opinion since I was the face to the market. I once experienced that a person from the Accountancy division suddenly started writing about performance measurement, and it was also rubbish. Of course this is very annoying because then suddenly [consulting firm] has two different stories on the market. (X1)

The situation in which a new management idea has already been formally settled within a particular unit may even hamper development efforts at other units. Obtaining a concept's formal ownership within a firm enables consultants to internally monopolize its development and exploitation. This means that everything associated with a new 'product', such as intakes, offers, further development efforts, and external marketing generally becomes coordinated by a dominant cluster that has been able to gain the most experience and power. A monopolizing unit may restrict others to developing and commercializing their own approach to a new management idea:

The label BPR is still in use within [consulting firm], only this concept belongs to the territory of another group. Not surprisingly such a situation can generate certain frictions [. . .]. (C2)

When different units are unable to monopolize a new commodified form of knowledge in a consultancy, development efforts may fuel conflicts about labeling. In this, different units may contest the vocabulary of a new idea. The outcome determines which terminology becomes acceptable to the different parties involved. Ultimately, these struggles may result in a situation in which different labels are coupled to similar 'products'. This allows different units to develop and control their own version without violating another's territory and prevent the firm suffering from cannibalization:

The labeling has been an elaborate discussion, mainly driven by politics. [. . .] We had a club, [consulting firm a], who had a strong position in organizational consulting and felt threatened by [consulting firm b] who, with a much larger volume, wanted to make a name for themselves on overlapping business. In spite of the fact that we were sister companies, it was considered as threatening, so the labeling caused a struggle even at the highest management level of our organization. If we suggested a label that was too much within the field of [a] they raised their hand and stressed that we should not do that. We have, for example, also thought about calling it Process Transformation, but that appeared to be a label that was not acceptable because [a] already used the term Transformation a lot. (F2)

Obstructed Implementation

In the previous section I indicated that new management ideas-in-development do not necessarily fit with a consultancy's institutionalized practices and therefore easily meet with substantial criticism and disbelief. This lack of perceived fit may not only affect the interpretation of an idea's value to a consulting firm, but also shape the actions that are associated with it in an interrelated way (see Table 5.1). In line with van de Ven (1986), a management idea can only become a successful new 'product' when it is implemented and thereby incorporated into an organization's shared patterns of thought and action. This means that a new management idea has to be appreciated and enacted by key organizational members to become established in a consultancy. Therefore, a lack of involvement constitutes an important problem base in linking development efforts to a consulting firm. As the data revealed, development efforts may suffer from an absence of internal support and collaboration, factors that are perceived to play an important role in the realization of a new knowledge product (Clark and Greatbatch, 2004). Our analysis indicates two important elements in relation to this issue. First, it shows that although consultancies may be eager to present themselves as innovative suppliers of management knowledge, a firm's management is not necessarily supportive of new commodification efforts:

> According to our management we could do something in the development of [product x], but we were not allowed to spend a substantial amount of time on it. We did not have the feeling that the managers really believed in the plan for the development of the method, they did not show any support for this, which resulted in the fact that at a certain moment it just faded out. (B2)

An important aspect for new commodified forms of knowledge to become accepted is the attitude of the management and their willingness to support the development of new ideas. A consultancy's management may not understand a new management idea or see its business opportunities. Not providing any space for putting a new knowledge product onto the market significantly hampers the process of commodification:

> That boss spoke the legendary words that we could do more useful things for [consulting firm] in our spare time, in other words, he was absolutely not enthusiastic about this concept. And as a result: At [consulting firm] I was strongly obstructed in doing development activities and research. (X1)

Second, the data also reveal that colleagues do not automatically understand the value of a new knowledge product for various reasons. The lack of support and collaboration resulting from this is regarded as a base that may significantly obstruct a new idea's implementation. The codification of management knowledge does not necessarily mean that a pioneering consultant's peers are able and willing to apply it in practice during their assignments. For instance, Burns and Stalker (1961) attributed the difficulties between what they call the 'laboratory' and the 'workshop' to linguistic problems. Specifically, they noted a systematic inability to translate new products from one specialist language to another. Also our consultant informants noted that within consultancies, attempts to transfer new knowledge 'products' from development to production are 'stranded' in problems of understanding, causing important barriers in the new ideas' realization and establishment. Efforts to incorporate new management ideas into the consultant's routines do not necessarily result in wider usage of this idea within a consulting firm when present consultants are not able to understand it:

> From the start, the BPR practice went prosperously and I acquired many of those projects, but unfortunately I had few colleagues that also were able to understand it. I had developed the BPR approach, but there was nobody at [consulting firm] left who was able to apply it. (N2)

A notable point made by Burns and Stalker (1961) is that they showed how the problems of understanding in the realization of innovations were generally embedded in larger political and status conflicts. Such conflicts are associated with different actors following their own interests, an issue that is regarded inherent to any new product development effort (Jones and Stevens, 1999). Our analysis revealed that although consultants are able to understand new forms of commodified knowledge, it does not necessarily become part of the taken-for-granted ideas and practices they draw upon during assignments. The data indicate that reluctance to incorporate a new management idea into established thoughts and action finds its origin in various reasons. The first reason is that establishment efforts within a consultancy likely encounter barriers of individual interests. This means that when a new idea is unable to contribute to perceived personal gains, consultants are less likely to be interested in using it. Obviously, a lack of interest on the 'receiving side' hampers the knowledge transfer process (Szulanski, 1996):

> The internal dissemination of a new concept within a consultancy generally gives a lot of trouble. [. . .] When consultants hear that they just have to apply it, maybe a few will obey, but most of them would rather not. [. . .] They continuously ask themselves whether it will help their career, whether it will fit their personality, what they can get out of it, and what is their own input. If the answer is that using a concept does not bring in much to them personally, they just don't do it. (T2)

A second motivation provided by the informants is that problems related to proprietary aspects of management knowledge not only appear on the market (Abbott, 1988; Fincham, 1995; Morris, 2001), but are also particularly apparent within a supplier of management knowledge. Although consultants may be working in the same firm and share similar professional interests, this does not necessarily guarantee cooperation in new commodification

ventures. As innovation theorists have already noted, a lack of coordina-
tion between different functions constitutes a major source of product development problems (Dougherty, 1996; Twiss, 1992) and easily generates
conflicts in achieving internal 'product consistency' (Clark and Fujimoto,
1991). Our interviews indicate that when commodification efforts related to
a similar knowledge 'product' are dispersed across a consultancy they easily compete with each other, thereby trying to define and protect their own
version of the idea:

> What generally happens is that when there is at a specific moment an
> interesting subject, a number of people likely dive in it. Sometimes this
> even happens at different locations in the agency. The Balanced Score-
> card has been taken up by people from Finance and Operations. Then
> a sound competition will start of people who find each other or delib-
> erately avoid each other and develop it independently. Eventually it will
> converge on a place where most experience arises. (C1)

As a result, efforts to develop a new management idea as a medium for
increased standardization across different units in a consultancy may easily lead to internal dissentions and objections. The dissemination of a new
'product' within a consultancy may specifically encounter barriers of departmental interests. Autonomous units that have invested in developing
their own repertoire are likely not eager to simply abandon their ideas and
practices in favor of a 'product' developed elsewhere:

> Moving from six different approaches to one single approach generated
> considerable friction at the expense of several people. [Consultant] has
> fallen victim to this. [. . .] That has been a considerable struggle because
> of course everyone had invested in their own approach and were not
> willing to simply throw these overboard. (P2)

Internal Legitimation

Our previous discussion of the data revealed that commodification is not
simply constructing a marketable knowledge product, but a process that
meets with considerable barriers that inhibit the establishment of a new idea
and underlying practices. In the perception of consultants, a key base related
to the establishment of new knowledge commodities is gaining legitimacy.
This indicates that the supply of management ideas is preceded by important
processes in which consultants have to sell their new 'products' internally
before they can sell them on the knowledge market. The knowledge-
intensive character of consultancies and their ideational products (Alvesson,
1993; Benders and van Veen, 2001; Clark, 1995) implies drawing heavily on
persuasive skills to internally legitimate new ideas in order to seduce people
to support and collaborate in developing novelty (see Table 5.2).

Table 5.2 Bases of legitimacy in commodification

Bases	Elements	Effects
Gaining legitimacy	• Presence and abilities of product champion • Receptive organizational climate • Persuasion of peers	Generation of potential to establishment of commodity

Arguably, the consultancy skills required to widely propagate new management ideas on the knowledge market (Bloomfield and Danieli, 1995; Pettigrew, 1975) are at least as necessary in new product development efforts within a consultancy. As one consultant noted:

> First you have to be able to convince the people internally before you can come out with it. [. . .] If you want to enlarge the initiative for product development and realize it in an organized setting, you have to convince the management that it is a good idea. (B2)

Gaining internal legitimacy for commodification efforts is related to the presence of a 'concept champion' and his ability to create a favorable impression (Stjernberg and Philips, 1993), thereby seducing people to support and collaborate in developing a new management idea. This means that in the realization of a knowledge 'product' it is regarded as important that there are people who believe in a new idea, propagate this belief, and seek to assemble a group of 'disciples' around it. Also such key persons are particularly able to acquire assignments and enhance enthusiasm through which the legitimation keeps up to a viable level:

> Often within a consultancy a concept champion emerges and it depends on his formal position, his charisma, the extent this person is able to inspire other consultants, and his commercial successes whether a concept may expand within a consulting firm. (K3)

Developing a new management idea may easily lose priority status in the absence of a champion that feels responsible for its realization. As some people obtained a position as concept champion it allowed them to further the development process of the new 'product' in their consulting firms. This enables a new idea to be led through the formal organization, thereby avoiding obstructing standards and procedures.

> In a sense I was the clergyman who preached BPR and thereby enthused people. [. . .] All through the firm I was regarded as Mr. BPR and this position enabled me to get certain things done. However, when I left the firm, a number of these things were strongly reduced. (P4)

At the same time, gaining legitimacy remains very dependent upon the ability of a champion to make a favorable impression. The success of this internal 'impression management' is perceived to be shaped by several key factors. First, in line with innovation theory (Brown and Ennew, 1995; Twiss, 1992), our informants emphasized the importance of a new management idea's market performance to overcome barriers of entry and gain internal recognition. When a new idea has 'proven' itself in praxis it will significantly enhance the appreciation of this idea within a consultancy.

> From the moment it was shown that the project in [client company] went very well you had something in hand to tell your group that this method is very interesting and could also be applied by other consultants. Because of the method's success other people become enthusiastic and it increasingly generates attention. (B1)

The prospects of satisfying identifiable consumer needs and commercial success likely increase the receptiveness of a consultancy to new management ideas. Therefore, to enhance a favorable reception, pioneering consultants may seek to convey the impression that new forms of commodified management knowledge are able to address contemporary problems in many client-organizations. So commercial and implementation successes increase the internal legitimation for a new idea and silence the critics:

> So BPR has been taken up by a number of people who strongly believed in it and with this belief were able to enthuse several clients to try it out. And because of a number of early successes they also started to propagate it internally. With this they gained a lot of credibility. [. . .] At a certain moment they convinced the rest of [consultancy] that BPR was a new way of thinking with which you could also make money. (Q1)

Second, the perceived success of a new knowledge 'product' in the marketplace is often not enough to become generally accepted. Rather, creating a receptive organizational climate is regarded as essential for a new management idea to be appreciated. In other words, the seed must also fall into fertile soil (Brown and Ennew, 1995; Deshpande and Zaltman, 1982) and has to become politically acceptable to a consultancy's management. The informants stressed that persuading managers to support and resource innovation projects is indissolubly linked with substantial internal promotional efforts. Such internal 'impression management' may involve emphasizing the strategic importance to a consultancy and presenting a new idea to conform with the consultancy's norms of talk and practice. In other words, pioneering consultants have to sell a new management idea to their management in order to bring it on to the market while they have to sell it outside to be able to establish it within a consultancy. Both the lack of a market prospects and internal promotional efforts will obstruct new commodified forms of management knowledge to gain legitimacy in a consultancy:

> Considering BPR, a number of enthusiastic people took it up and got the space to further develop it and do assignments. Actually we have been successful because we brought in a large assignment with which we were able to show that we were also profitable. Gradually the conviction grew that there was a market for it so then you may proceed. [. . .] If there is no such belief or conviction, it is going to be very difficult. (W2)

Third, a major complication in the establishment and success of a new knowledge 'product' is that it cannot be separated from the consultants who are applying it (Clark, 1995; Visscher, 2001). For new commodified forms of knowledge to become institutionalized within a consultancy it is regarded as crucial to win the acceptance of colleague consultants. Persuading their peers to incorporate novel ideas into their daily practices requires commodification efforts that are accompanied by training programs aimed at educating colleagues and supporting them in applying the repertoire. This not only increases their peers' knowledge of novelty, but also enhances internal acceptance, thereby reducing resistance to changes associated with innovations.

> In this case you saw that something nice was developed at a central level, after which these ideas were pulled out of this central unit. That course is run every month, is fully booked, and there is a waiting list. In addition, people will apply it in projects, achieve commercial successes and in this way it can disseminate within the organization. It just happens this way in our firm, not by anyone saying that from now on you have to do Process Development this way, because nobody would care about that. (F2)

Consultancies increase the likelihood of winning the acceptance of peers by following an integrated commodification process (Clark and Fujimoto, 1991). In this they develop a knowledge 'product' into a common standardized language (Werr, 1999), while at the same time increasing consultants' involvement in the development process. This offers the possibility for co-development, thereby allowing consultants to include their own ideas and give the new idea a personal interpretation under the veil of tailoring their services to an individual client's requirements (Clark, 1995). So persuading peers mainly involves emphasizing the advantages of an elaborately developed standardized repertoire while allowing for the possibility of context-specific adaptations:

So as [consultancy T] we encourage consultants to make the method tailor-made to the client situation. This brings two important things. First, that person who brings it to the client has the feeling that it's partly his own work. It is not something that he simply got from the consultancy, but also includes his own input. Second, the client has the feeling that he is not getting something general from [consultancy T] but is buying a concept that has been specifically made for his industry. [. . .] This does mean that you will get 5,000 variations on each method, and we accept that. Those variations are generally not inspired by their own opinion but because consultants believe that their client is different. If people need this to justify their own interpretation, I'll buy that. Basically a consultant wants to put his personal mark on a concept because that is related to his ego. With this you want to show that you are unique. (T1)

CONCLUSION

This chapter draws on the product innovation literature to examine the struggles inherent in the development of new knowledge products within management knowledge entrepreneurs. Theorists of product innovation have persistently emphasized that the development of novelty within organizations is unavoidably a source of problems (Dougherty, 1996; van de Ven, 1986). It is argued that new product development does not fit institutionalized organizational practices and therefore theorists stress the importance of legitimation efforts to satisfy internal demands. Therefore I explored the possibility of viewing knowledge commodification as a contested process within the system of management knowledge supply. Using interviews with management consultants, I analyzed the intraorganizational elements that may inhibit or encourage the development of new knowledge 'products'. Thus rather than regarding the process of commodification as a linear and straightforward series of logical steps that start with generating promising ideas and result in a knowledge product's market launch or assuming that this process is automatically supported by various collaborative relationships, this chapter shows that consultants as knowledge entrepreneurs regard this process as particularly problematic. It indicates that there are a number of important factors that inhibit the development of new management ideas.

First, I found that consultants perceive major impediments to linking a new management idea to their firms' strategy and resources. As a result, developing new ideas do not necessarily fit with established practices and do not automatically enjoy support and collaboration within knowledge entrepreneurs. The incompatibility of a new idea with the current product range of a consultancy is considered highly problematic, and a major reason for criticism and disbelief, irrespective of its intrinsic merits. This means that within a consultancy, elements such as established and institutionalized consulting practices, perceived inconsistency of an idea with the image of a firm, and possibility of cannibalization violating an established practice area or territory of a specific group within a consultancy may constitute considerable barriers to the emergence and development of new management ideas.

Second, another base of struggles related to the internal establishment of new management ideas within consultancies relates to the lack of agency and involvement of a consultancy's management and of other organizational members. As the analysis has shown, development efforts may suffer from an absence of internal support and collaboration—factors that play an important role in the establishment of a new knowledge product. This entails that a consultancy's management is not necessarily supportive of new management ideas and that different consultants within a firm do not automatically understand the value of a new idea. Indeed the abstraction, codification, and translation of management knowledge in a new knowledge 'product' does not necessarily mean that the peers of the pioneering consultant are able and willing to apply it in practice during their assignments. Thus although consultants may be working in the same firm and share similar professional interests, this does not necessarily guarantee cooperation in commodification ventures.

6 Practicing and Preaching

The previous two chapters explored dimensions 'internal' to a consultancy that play a role in shaping the 'social life' of a commodity. But how do knowledge entrepreneurs 'practice' the management ideas they preach? In this chapter I will zoom in on external dimensions and in particular how consultants understand the enactment of commodified forms of management knowledge in relation to their assignments. This is relevant because it allows further insight into the way ideas are appropriated, enacted, and adapted beyond their moment of exchange and how these activities feed into the ongoing processes of producing and dislocating management knowledge (Heusinkveld et al., 2011), or as Kopytoff stressed, 'the fact that an object is bought or exchanged says nothing about its subsequent status and whether it will remain a commodity or not' (1986: 76). Therefore this chapter may contribute to addressing a wider central concern in management research about the possible impact of these commodified forms of management knowledge on management and organizational practice (Clark, 2004; Røvik, 2011; Sturdy, 2004, 2011).

Prior literature has provided important insights into how management knowledge commodities are created (Anand et al., 2007; Heusinkveld and Benders, 2005) and their main functions for knowledge entrepreneurs in relation to potential clients (Kieser, 2002; Morris, 2001; Werr et al., 1997; Whittle, 2006). Yet we know relatively little about how knowledge entrepreneurs enact the ideas they sell (Reihlen and Nikolova, 2010; Wright and Kitay, 2004), beyond the assumption that they use these 'products' pragmatically in consulting assignments (Benders et al., 1998; Berglund and Werr, 2000; Furusten, 2009; Morris, 2001; Whittle, 2005) and adjust them to fit the organizational context (Strang and Meyer, 1993; Benders and van Veen, 2001; Suddaby and Greenwood, 2001). As Werr realizes, 'the application of this knowledge is not generally discussed' (2002: 104; see also Clark, 2004; Røvik, 2011; Whittle, 2006). This is an important gap because the translation of these abstracted and codified forms of knowledge into local action is an essential stage in the commodification of management knowledge (Czarniawska and Sevón, 1996; Suddaby and Greenwood, 2001) and likely crucial for a successful consulting assignment (Morris, 2001; Werr et al., 1997). In addition, enacting consultancy-induced concepts has significant consequences not just for the client organizations (Grint and Case, 1998; O'Shea and Madigan, 1997), but also for managing the consulting firm's workforce (Løwendahl and Revang, 2004).

To advance insights into the enactment of commodified forms of management knowledge, in terms of the translation of abstract, codified concepts into local action, I draw on a practice-based perspective. Accordingly, I seek a richer theoretical understanding of the way human agents understand the logics of social practices that shape the way 'rule-following' takes place (Jarzabkowski, 2004; Schön, 1983; Tsoukas, 1996). To understand these logics in relation to management knowledge commodification, I focus on the frames established by consultants, that is, the interpretative schemes they use to make sense of and justify possible translations of their commodified forms of management knowledge in their assignments (Cornelissen et al., 2011; Schön, 1983). On the basis of the interviews with management consultants, this chapter identifies key framing moves related to dispositional and interactive-situational dimensions that consultants use to make sense of and justify the possible translations of management ideas in their assignments. These framing moves provide a broader theoretical understanding of relevant processes that shape management knowledge commodification and clarify important preconditions that may limit possible alternative interpretations.

In the next section, I first posit that the way consultants construct a management idea in relation to a client-consultant relationship offers a relevant research context. Then I outline a practice-based perspective that may provide a clearer understanding of the logic of social practices that underlies the enactment of management ideas. Subsequently, I present the results of the empirical analysis and detail key framing moves that may encourage or inhibit possible translations of management ideas. Finally, I discuss theoretical implications of the analysis and suggest fruitful directions for research.

RESEARCH CONTEXT: CLIENT-CONSULTANT RELATIONSHIP

Consultants are relevant knowledge entrepreneurs because they not only influence the supply of management ideas (Faust, 2002; Furusten, 1999), but also are deeply involved in actual change projects induced by or associated with these commodified forms of management knowledge (O'Shea and Madigan, 1997; Wright and Kitay, 2004). An in-depth study of how consultants construct a concept in relation to a client-consultant relationship may provide further insights into how these management knowledge commodities get translated into practice.

First, client-consultant relations are important settings for the conduct of consulting work. Consultants do not develop their services in isolation, but rather produce them as outcomes of processes of interaction or coproduction with their clients (Clark, 1995; Reihlen and Nikolova, 2010; Sturdy et al., 2009). Theorists draw on different perspectives to conceptualize the differences between consultants and clients and the related complexities that shape the consultancy process. Early, more functionalist work has understood these differences in terms of a fundamental discrepancy between the professional values of the consultant and those that prevail in the client organization (Argyris, 1961). More recent studies relate divergences between client and consultant to mechanism of power (Fincham, 1999), role-related expectations (Hislop, 2002), information asymmetries (Sharma, 1997), social boundaries (Kitay and Wright, 2004), or communication systems (Mohe and Seidl, 2011). In addition, theorists have emphasized that the concept of the client does not imply a homogeneous, stable entity (Fincham, 2012; Sturdy et al., 2009). Instead, in the production of services, consultants deal with a 'heterogeneous assemblage' (Alvesson et al., 2009: 253) of client roles and interests that vary not only by project, but also over time as the project evolves (Sturdy et al., 2009).

Second, processes of framing play a key role in consultants' interactions with clients. Frames determine how the consultancy service takes shape and constitute the relation itself (Clark, 1995; Coupland et al., 1994; Sturdy, 1997). Recent studies thus depict client-consultant relations in a state of constant indeterminacy, within which boundaries constantly get negotiated and reframed as the consulting project unfolds (Czarniawska and Mazza, 2003; Fincham, 1999; Pellegrini, 2002; Sturdy et al., 2009). Consultants' sociopolitical skills and particularly their use of language have special significance for shaping managers' meanings (Bloomfield and Danieli, 1995; Nikolova et al., 2009). They discursively frame problems and solutions to ensure they are acceptable and remove possible client uncertainties or anxieties (Clark, 1995; Sturdy, 1997). In the words of Bloomfield and Vurdubakis (1994: 455), consultants 'represent reality in order to act on it, control or dominate it, as well as to secure the compliance of others in that domination.'

In light of these motives, I argue that the way consultants frame a management idea as an enacted practice in relation to a client-consultant relationship is theoretically relevant for describing its translation into local action. By focusing on frames used by consultants, I highlight only one side of the story, but considering their widespread involvement in the dissemination and application of management knowledge commodities in organizations, I believe this focus constitutes a necessary and important step to shed more light on the possible impact of knowledge entrepreneurs and their ideas on management and organizational practice.

A PRACTICE-BASED PERSPECTIVE

The study of practices comprises various approaches in distinct fields (Miettinen et al., 2009), though practice-based theory generally addresses how relevant social actors construct the manner in which they 'engage in rule-bound practical activities' (Tsoukas, 1996: 13). Understanding the enactment of a concept thus involves considering the logic of social activity within which rule-following occurs (Bourdieu, 1990; Jarzabkowski, 2004; Schön, 1983; Whittington, 2006). For this research, these perspectives suggest that the social activity that may enhance or inhibit possibilities for translating ideas into practice consists of two key dimensions: a dispositional dimension and an interactive-situational dimension.

First, practice-based theorists suggest that the dispositional dimension, or practitioners' habitus, plays an important role in understanding the specific interpretation and enactment of new problem situations or solutions. According to Tsoukas (1996: 17), organizational members' knowledge repertoires consist of 'past socializations.' This entails that iterative cycles of prior enactment and sensemaking ultimately lead to the development of habitualized thinking and acting in response to specific organizational problems or solutions (Bourdieu, 1990). Engaging in social practices influences the practitioner's cognitive schemata, which constitute a basis for and set limits on new enactments (Jarzabkowski, 2004; Orlikowski, 2002; Tsoukas, 1996). In Schön's (1983) description, practitioners rely on past experience to recognize that a new problem situation is of a certain kind, and then choose the proper frame for it. Naming the situation entails a process of 'seeing-as,' which means recognizing the new situation as a variation of previously encountered situations, and then 'doing-as' by acting in parallel with actions taken in the former situation. On an organizational level, these acquired routinized patterns of thinking and acting guide actions and assessments of problem situations and solutions (Feldman and Pentland, 2003; Howard-Grenville, 2005).

Thus, from a practice-based perspective, differences in the interpretation and enactment of practices stem from practitioners' distinct histories (Bourdieu, 1990: 54) and prior knowledge. In turn, the prior possession of knowledge increases the likelihood that relevant new ideas and practices get readily accepted and used (Howard-Grenville, 2005). Moreover, a broader and more elaborate knowledge repertoire allows the practitioners to take less exploratory routes or shortcuts toward the recognition and application of new knowledge and technology (March, 1981). Cohen and Levinthal (1990: 131) refer to this situation as 'insight,' or the 'rapid solution of a problem' that is possible because of the availability of prior knowledge. Practitioners with more prior knowledge likely take shortcuts because their 'preparedness' enables them to understand and use new practices more readily.

Second, practice-based approaches indicate that to understand the enactment of practices in action, we must consider the specific interactive-situational dimension that activates the practitioner's past socializations or dispositions (Jarzabkowski et al., 2007; Orlikowski, 2002; Tsoukas, 1996; Whittington, 2006). In line with Bourdieu (1990), practice-based theorists emphasize that the enactment of practices depends on how practitioners experience the interactive situation and assess conditions for further enactment (Whittington, 2006). That is, 'Agents' choices will be influenced by their consideration of what is possible' (Jarzabkowski, 2004: 532). Schön (1983) describes this process as a 'reflective conversation with the situation,' which begins with the frame or interpretative scheme that the practitioner uses to make sense of a situation and establish a basis for action (cf. Cornelissen et al., 2011). Thus the situation gets adapted to the frame, 'through a web of moves' (Schön, 1983: 131) that help the practitioner explore and evaluate the frame's consequences and necessary conditions (Visscher and Fisscher, 2009). In a process of pragmatic experimentation, a unique situation is then 'understood through the attempt to change it' (Schön, 1983: 132). On an organizational level, it thus relates to what Feldman and Pentland (2003) call the 'performative aspect' of routines. A specific situation informs practitioners how to enact and reenact their acquired routines (Howard-Grenville, 2005). Because the enactment of practices is always local, it cannot be known completely ex ante, but it is 'inherently indeterminate' (Tsoukas, 1996: 22).

Thus, from a practice-based perspective, the enactment of prior experiences also relates to actors' understanding of the possibilities offered by local circumstances. Through reflection on the intended and unintended consequences of the initial frame, actors use, adapt, or reproduce specific practices (Whittington, 2006). If these conditions appear favorable, 'habitual, routinized use may be expected' (Jarzabkowski, 2004: 544) which could pave the way to shortcuts that offer opportunities for realizing more radical changes (Visscher and Visscher-Voerman, 2010). However, the possible interpretations of a practice also may be restricted if actors' intended uses deviate from the possibilities of the 'immediate circumstances and local agendas' (Tsoukas, 1996: 20).

In turn, I argue that to better understand the possible impact of knowledge entrepreneurs and their commodified forms of management knowledge on management and organizational practice, one needs to examine how consultants frame management ideas as enacted practices. Informed by practice-based approaches, I seek to explore empirically how consultants' framing moves, related to their dispositions and perceptions of what is feasible in a specific situation, encourage or inhibit possible translations of management ideas within the context of a consulting assignment.

FRAMING IDEAS AS ENACTED PRACTICE

To determine how consultants frame a management concept as enacted practice, I explored how they constructed management concepts in relation to assignments in client organizations. Using a practice lens, I detail how commodified forms of management knowledge are not only the outcome of a series of distinct phases that result in a management concept to be sold on the management knowledge market or standards to guide practice, they also should be understood as enacted practice. In the analysis of the interview data, I concentrated on how consultants frame their enactment of management concepts in practice to identify the elements these consultants used as a rationale for their framing. Specifically, this analysis revealed key frames pertaining to dispositional and interactive-situational dimensions that consultants use to make sense of and justify the possible translation of management concepts in their assignments. These frames limit or encourage a view of a management concept as an open-ended practice (see Table 6.1), as I discuss next.

Dispositional Dimension

Related to the dispositional dimension I identify two relevant categories of framing moves that consultants use to shape legitimate courses of action for translating commodified forms of management knowledge, namely, (1) experiential insights and (2) collective routines.

Framing Category 1: Experiential Insights
This first key category relates to a consultant's personal experiences. To frame management ideas as enacted practice, consultants draw on arguments associated with their individual past socializations. Thus the habits of thinking that a consultant has developed over time through involvement in previous social practices offer arguments to encourage or limit the perception of a management idea as an open-ended practice. This frame may imply moves related to both (a) familiarity with a management idea, and (b) the level of seniority. First, consultants achieve substantial experience with particular knowledge 'products' and use this familiarity to argue for a reduction in the number of potential alternative routes. Our informants suggested that reflecting on the insights generated in their past socializations helps them see and legitimize shortcuts to translate a management idea to an application within a client organization. For example:

> . . . clients often would like to have an elaborate preassessment, but we now only perform a short version. On the basis of our experience we can see very quickly what is necessary to start a BPR trajectory. It does not make any sense to write things out elaborately when I know them already after two meetings. (N1)

On the flip side, the consultants framed a lack of experience with the application of a specific idea as an important motivation to leave more alternatives open during the advice trajectory. This is characterized by one of the interviewees as follows:

Table 6.1 Overview of framing moves

Dimension	Framing categories	Conception of moves	Framing moves	
			Moves inhibiting viewing management idea as open-ended practice	Moves encouraging viewing management idea as open-ended practice
Dispositional	1. Experiential insights	Using the involvement in previous social practices as rationale to make sense of and justify the possible translations of a management idea	• Familiarity with idea • Lower levels of seniority	• Less familiarity with idea • Higher levels of seniority
	2. Collective routines	Using the routines that are shared with colleagues from the same firm as rationale to make sense of and justify the possible translations of a management idea	• Focused methodic repertoire • Specialist position/ reputation	• Open methodic repertoire • Generalist position/ reputation
Interactive-situational	3. Client interpretive schemes	Using the way clients understand a management concept as rationale to make sense of and justify the possible translations of a management idea	• Narrow question • Predefined understanding of idea • Substantial ambition/ commitment	• Open question • Flexible understanding of idea • Low ambition/ commitment
	4. Organizational setting	Presenting the sociotemporal context of the client organization as rationale to make sense of and justify the possible translations of a management idea	• Short-term client relations • Significant pressures to client organization • Simple problem situation	• Long-term client relations • Fewer pressures to client organization • Complex problem situation

In early instances we came to the client with a number of vague pictures and together with that client we learned a lot. At that moment you are just looking for a number of early adopters of that BPR concept . . . After a while, the concept has been much more detailed into methods, techniques, and tools. (Q2)

Second, the category of experiential insights was also associated with seniority, or a state of having obtained more or less general experience in the consultancy occupation. Our consultant informants used a low degree of seniority to frame the limits on the range of alternative courses of action when constructing a management idea as enacted practice:

The board of directors of a large Dutch company asked me to do a project and one of the final stages concerned convincing the Worker's Council. They were with 20 men and asked about my way of working. After I indicated that I would start with a couple of interviews, they particularly asked whether I would do my interviews with standardized questionnaires. I said that this was certainly not the case, and a short time later I heard I was allowed to do the project. Apparently earlier consultancies indicated that they planned to send a book with a questionnaire and would draw conclusions, only on the basis of the outcome of such a questionnaire. So by uniforming and standardizing they thought they could compensate for a lack of experience from the consultants. In my view, a key question is to what extent, in this case, can BPR still be characterized as organizational advice? (P1)

In contrast, a higher level of seniority motivates a broader number of alternative options in the translation of an idea in a consultancy assignment. In such a case, the informants framed the enactment as less predetermined and more exploratory. As one consultant put it:

Indeed, also in our consultancy various clusters of tools and techniques emerge so that people can address certain issues in a more standardized way. But where Gemini, BCG, and certainly McKinsey with their Overhead Value Analysis had developed a manual that had to be followed rather strictly, such an approach would clearly not work at our consultancy. We hire a lot of experienced people directly from industry who don't accept using such a cookbook and don't like to be put in a straitjacket of a specific solution pattern. (A1)

Framing Category 2: Collective Routines

When framing management ideas as enacted practice, I found that collective routines within the firm provide a motive to limit or encourage more exploratory courses of action. I found framing categories associated with (a) perceived stringency of a dominant firm repertoire, but also (b) breadth of the repertoire. First, the analysis revealed that the amount of focus associated with a specific consulting repertoire is systematically associated with the degree of freedom inherent to the repertoire, as used by a particular consultancy, which then relates to possibilities for taking more or less exploratory routes in the translation of an idea. Consultants framed a more focused repertoire as an important rationale for encouraging less open-ended translations, thereby restricting any alternative routes considered in an advice trajectory. For example:

> Yesterday I read that consultancies will do anything to meet the clients' preferences. However I do not really recognize this in our practice. Of course, the client is central, but *we* know how to redesign organizations. No, I don't recognize this so much, but this might have to do with [consultancy] and their specific positioning in the market. At [consultancy] we will say this is the way we do BPR and this is the way we know [it] will be the best way. Of course you will discuss this with your client, but ultimately we will do it our way and your employees can participate in our team. So you could say that this approach is rather coercive. Of course a client could say, 'can't we do this in four months instead of six?' and then we will probably agree on five months. But these are just marginal issues. (L2)

In other instances, consultants understood a more open methodology as a legitimate motivation to allow for more alternative routes in an idea's translation. One interviewee thus noted the role of repertoire in framing a management idea as enacted practice:

> Previously, our client offer [concerning BPR] included a very detailed weekly planning. We made this detailed planning on the basis of one or maybe two talks with a board of directors. Currently, we have agreed that we only define a detailed first step with the client and on the basis of this see how we will continue, thereby leaving our role more open-ended. So we just offer less to clients who look for certainty in terms of methods. This entails that we should offer more certainty in terms of trust or explain that this certainty will only increase during the next steps. (V1)

Second, collective routines are also associated with the strategic positioning of the consultancy. Being positioned as a specialist is used as an important move to constrain the number of available options in the translation, whereas a more generalist repertoire offered a means to limit the possible view of commodified forms of knowledge as open-ended practice and thereby enlarged the number of possible options. If associated with consultancies that draw on an all-purpose method, a management idea as enacted practice would be represented as more indefinite. Two informants aptly summarized these conflicting positions:

> A firm such as [consultancy] had a rather strategic approach to BPR and the method that we used drew heavily on this perspective. This approach did not lend itself to implement small improvements on the department level or application level. However, such an operational approach became dominant on the market and involved the largest number of consulting assignments. I discussed this development in my article 'Ten ways to mess up Redesign'. (Q2)
>
> We particularly identify ourselves with client questions about more integral problems, which entails building bridges between different disciplines. Although different elements are included in our assignments, we are not IT specialists, neither are we typical HRM consultants nor consultants who primarily focus on implementing new control systems including performance measurement. We feel well up when different interrelated aspects are considered and we have to balance them. (V1)

Interactive-Situational Dimension

The second dimension also comprises two distinct categories of framing moves that consultants use to rationalize their translations of a management idea, namely (3) client interpretative schemes and (4) organizational setting.

Framing Category 3: Client Interpretative Schemes
Consultants stressed the significance of considering how the client makes sense of a management idea to frame it as enacted practice. This became particularly apparent when they associated a management idea's translation with (a) the key question being asked of the consultant, (b) the client's initial interpretation of the idea, and (c) the client's sophistication and commitment. First, I found that the central question that confronts consultants in their initial talks with clients is seen as important in framing the management idea as enacted practice. Specifically, a narrow client question offered a rationale for reducing the number of available courses of action, as one managing consultant noted:

> I noticed that BPR became a proper name and every company thought that they should have applied it. It sometimes occurred that a client contacted us with the question: 'we would like you to do BPR here.' For a consultant this is the most horrifying question. It would be the same if someone who is deadly ill calls the doctor and asks him to give him a specific pill. Obviously that doctor first wants to make an exact diagnosis and determine the kind of medicine himself. Of course you are going to talk to that client; it would be not very clever if you would immediately say we don't do that. (W1)

Consultants instead used broader client questions as a motive to promote a more open-ended view of the idea's translation and support more exploratory routes in their assignment. For example:

> One question that was asked by clients was whether we could tell about BPR and why organizations should adopt this concept. In such a case, you could use those client questions about BPR to talk about the underlying problems of the organization in order to sell your services. (J1)

Second, clients might have predefined interpretations of a management idea, developed prior to their contacts with the consultant. The consultants then framed this client-specific reading of an idea as a relevant motive to enhance or restrict possible alternative routes. If they perceived the clients' interpretations as narrow, they framed them as constraining the number of optional courses of action, as illustrated in the following excerpt:

> We were asked by a large insurance company. We did a presentation about BPR showing all our experiences and emphasized the possibilities and limitations of using the concept. Later we heard that we did not get the assignment because the board of directors considered our ideas about BPR too modest. The consultancy that presented shortly after we gave our presentation was more in line with the approach to BPR that this client was looking for. I wished them good luck but did not expect much because that's not the way it works in practice. That client associated BPR with revolutionary chances, but this was not included in our approach. (W1)

But consultants also used more open-ended interpretations among clients to frame the translation of the management idea as less restricted. That is, more indefinite client understanding served as a justification for opening courses of action that otherwise might have been closed:

> A good example is that we are currently redesigning the call-center processes of an insurance company. That client indicated that, in principle, all of the current processes including legacy systems may be redesigned. So we could redesign everything including front office and mid-office without any restrictions. (K2)

Third, the client's interpretative scheme is also associated with the use of client ambition or capacity as framing moves. Consultants constructed starting conditions, in terms of the client's own strength and commitment, to frame the possible translation of a management idea in an assignment. That is, a strong, committed client served as motivation to frame a management idea as a relatively straightforward enacted practice that encouraged ambitious solutions and shortcuts in the process. One of the consultant interviewees explained:

A common element in the projects I performed was that generally a standard phasing emerged which in terms of approach and content was dependent on the specific client situation. An important aspect concerned the top management of a client organization: how far would they go and to what extent are they able to deal with these changes? For me it is not particularly difficult to strictly follow our approach in which every step that should be taken is explained in detail, but in practice you have to deal with uncertainty such as the capacity of the top management. (P2)

In contrast, a judgment of a management idea as too ambitious or too hard to implement would be used to encourage a more open-ended translation. The above quote indicates that the absence of strong management to implement BPR can be used as a rationale for reframing the situation as one in which the organization needed fine-tuning to its current structure and a stronger market orientation. Thus consultants may associate the absence of starting conditions with a more open-ended framing of the idea as enacted practice, which encouraged the exploration of alternative directions in the problem-solving process.

Framing Category 4: Organizational Setting
The organizational setting category implied that consultants used motivations related to a specific sociotemporal context in the client organization to encourage or limit the possibility of framing a management idea as an open-ended practice. This category encompasses three aspects: (a) client relations, (b) pressures experienced by the client organization, and (c) complexity of the problem situation. First, our analysis indicated that the perceived strength of the client-consultant relationship offered an important reason to limit or enhance the framing of a management idea as an open-ended practice. Our informants thus indicated that a weak relationship with a client provided a rationale for narrowing the number of alternative routes. This is illustrated as follows:

In a number of cases, managers were assigned to lead a change within a client organization. But in case these managers were sacked and our firm [consultancy K] was seen as his ally, we automatically lost legitimacy which also negatively affected the change program. Organizations are political arenas and managers do not necessarily act in the best interest of their company. If you are in such a situation as a consultancy, you have to make sure that you will go out unharmed and make clear to the people in the client organization that you have not deceived them. (K3)

Framing an idea as an open-ended practice was more likely when consultants could point to a closer relationship with the client organization. For example, one managing consultant revealed that the strength of his relationship with a particular client offered an important argument to pursue a more ambitious, exploratory trajectory:

> I did a BPR assignment at a large telecom company which aimed at realizing a cost reduction of 25%. The contact with the project leader was really perfect and allowed us to take additional risks by increasing the ambition level. We even suggested cutting parts of the control department. For that company it was quite revolutionary to say that these people should do something else. But as a consultant you can only say this when you have a good relationship with your project leader. So not only the style of the consultant, but also his relationship with the client, determine the way a project takes shape. (T1)

Second, another concept related to organization setting pertained to the pressures on the client organization. The consultants used the demands confronting their clients to frame or reframe a management idea as enacted practice, such as by emphasizing the significance of time pressures to narrow down the optional routes considered in a consulting assignment:

> I did a project that lasted about eight years from initiation until implementation, while in terms of organizational structure I did exactly the same in a client organization of about the same size in nine months. Obviously this does not mean that relevant aspects such as attitude and behavior have changed yet, but the structure has been changed radically. Indeed, some companies do not feel the necessity so much and, as a result, these projects may suffer from substantial delays. Hence, the variation I experienced in those projects could be easily related to the top management and the pressure of their business; in fact this does not only apply to BPR projects, but also to any consulting assignment. (P2)

Or another consultant related the pressures experienced by clients to specific sectors (see also Fincham et al., 2008):

> While the specific sector does not really matter whether you will adopt a specific method or not, it plays a crucial role in the way you interpret this method. For instance in Health care you just have to develop much more patience during the whole trajectory. Something you can achieve in the private sector organizations within four months just isn't possible in Health care. Within Hospitals I would typify BPR as designing something new, but subsequently following a more gradual implementation trajectory of a model that is very roughly seen as endpoint. Strictly this cannot be considered as an old-fashioned BPR trajectory because it just needs much more time. (V3)

In a similar way, the consultant informants draw on cases with less time pressures to frame the translation of the idea in more open-ended ways to encourage more exploratory trajectories. For instance:

> If a client would have more time we don't call it BPR, but Enterprise Reengineering. In that case you will consider the systems, the strategic impact, and positioning of the client organization in the market. In terms of ambition you will say that the client should enhance their service levels or reduce costs drastically to remain competitive in the long run. If the client would even have more time, then you would focus more on cultural issues and phrase it in terms of that the client should adapt the behaviors of their employees, thereby enhancing their passion, discipline, and the learning abilities of the organization. (R1)

Finally, some framing moves drew on the cognitive and sociopolitical complexity of the exact problem. I found that consultants used relatively simple situations as a motive to associate a management idea as enacted practice with taking shortcuts in their analysis; one consultant claimed that a well-managed organization allowed him to translate the management idea straightforwardly:

> A very remarkable finding was that you could apply BPR very well to a well-managed organization that maximizes the possibilities within an existing process design. In the Netherlands, [company X] was a good example because it has with the 'Today for tomorrow' project totally redesigned their business processes, but from a very stable and very well-managed organization. (Q2)

However, complex situations provided reasons to frame the translation of a management idea as a more open-ended enterprise: more carefully, with more exploration, and more reflectively. The informants associated a more straightforward framing of a management idea as enacted practice in such politically complex cases with a premature termination of the problem analysis, a loss of commitment, and severe implementation problems. As one consultant explained:

> Another category of [BPR] projects did not follow our approach completely or has narrowed down this approach to only an IT implementation trajectory. When examining the reasons for this we found that this typically occurred in client organizations that faced substantial difficulties and were forced to make large-scale changes. I have experienced coups of board members against the chairman and I have seen how support for change crumbled because the members

of the board of directors weren't able to change themselves in spite of the fact that the company's staff was very enthusiastic. It appeared that in such cases top management tried to obstruct the changes or sought to narrow down or simplify our project which entailed that failure was built-in because it no longer complied with the necessary conditions. (K3)

CONCLUSION

Using a practice-based perspective, this chapter explored how knowledge entrepreneurs practice the management ideas they preach. The analysis in this chapter has revealed that framing commodified forms of knowledge as enacted practice relates to two core dimensions: dispositional and interactive-situational. Each dimension comprises several key framing moves that the consultants mobilize to make sense of and justify their translation of a management idea in the context of that specific assignment. These moves may encourage or inhibit a view of a management idea as open-ended practice.

First, along the dispositional dimension, consultants used their experiential insights and collective routines as rationales to make sense of and justify their translations of a management idea. They sought to inhibit frames of an idea as open-ended practice by associating its translation with high familiarity, low seniority, a more focused repertoire, and specialist positioning. Similarly, consultants drew on disposition-related motives such as less familiarity, more seniority, an open repertoire, and a generalist positioning to encourage more open-ended translations of commodified forms of management knowledge during a particular assignment.

Second, I found that consultants use clients' interpretative schemes and local organizational settings to make sense of and justify the possible translations of a management idea. I have outlined various framing moves consultants used to inhibit a view of a management idea as open-ended, such as relating the idea to a relatively simple problem situation sparked by a narrow client question, and highlighting higher levels of ambition in and pressures on the client organization. Consultants instead drew on interactive-situational reasons to promote a more open-ended translation when they related the management idea as enacted practice to a complex problem situation that initiated with an open-ended client question, described their more flexible understanding of the idea, and experienced little pressure.

Third, although I stressed how framing moves encourage either predetermined or more open-ended translations, this does not mean that they always align in any specific assignment. The consultants rather made clear that it is always possible that frames contradict one another and create tensions, dilemmas, and trade-offs. For instance, a consultant may limit the possibility to frame the enactment of a management idea as open-ended when it is embraced simultaneously by the client and the consultant, the problem situation is relatively simple, the sociopolitical conditions are favorable to making shortcuts, and the consultant has a suitable repertoire as well as the knowledge and experience to implement the idea.

Typically, the enactment of a management idea may be encouraged to be framed as open-ended only when the situation is particularly complex, there is little experience with the specific problem and little knowledge about the organization concerned, a high level of trust in the capacities and commitment of the client, plenty of time resources, and the repertoire of the consultant can accommodate a large variety of possible routes in the process. However, the comments of the consultants made clear that in many cases this process of framing is not particularly straightforward: relevant elements will not point in the same direction, will have an influence on each other, and may not have the same significance in different situations.

7   Stretching Cycles

In seeking to shed new light on the production of 'new' management ideas the preceding chapters in this book have indicated the significance of considering different spheres prior to and after the market exchange in which commodified forms of management knowledge may reside. This chapter takes a longitudinal perspective to analyze how the evolving supply-side dynamics shape the 'biography' of knowledge commodities. Indeed, a contested issue in current research pertains to what happens after an idea's popularity declines: does it die or does it stay (Abrahamson and Fairchild, 1999; Clark, 2004; O'Mahoney, 2007; Perkmann and Spicer, 2008; Røvik, 2011; Spell, 2001)? Most studies focus on the early stages in the 'lives' of a management idea and primarily on the way these commodified forms of management knowledge are produced so as to be inherently attractive and accessible to managers (Clark, 2004; Clark and Greatbatch, 2004). But research offers less detail about the supply-side dynamics that arise after the initial stages beyond the assumption that these ideas are either abandoned or maintained as a result of their (lack of) legitimacy on the management knowledge market (Abrahamson and Fairchild, 1999; David and Strang, 2006; Suddaby and Greenwood, 2001), or that 'old' ideas may be reiterated as new commodities (Abrahamson and Eisenman, 2008; Guillén, 1994). Suddaby and Greenwood stress that the commodification of management knowledge unavoidably entails a 'spiraling need for new ideas and practices that can be commodified and sold' (2001: 945) and even suggest that the pace of commodification is quickening, resulting in 'hypercompetition' (2001: 945) among management knowledge entrepreneurs. Whatever the case, prior analyses cannot explain how and why management ideas are reshaped over time, or remain unclear about how population-level life cycle models relate to firm-level dynamics. This is an important gap in the literature on management ideas because such supply-side dynamics shape the way commodified forms of management knowledge evolve and how management knowledge may survive a fashion boom and bust on the market.

To contribute to prior literature on the role of the supply-side dynamics in the evolution of commodified forms of management knowledge, this chapter investigates how management consultants respond after the initial phase in the life of a commodity in the market, and especially when an initially popular commodity goes out of vogue. Therefore, the central research question in this chapter is: how do consultancies respond to competing pressures in the maturity and decline phases of a new management idea in the market? To address this question I adopt an institutional perspective because it allows furthering of our understanding about how fashion setters respond to multiple pressures (Deephouse, 1999; Oliver, 1991; Pache and Santos, 2010). Using interview and print media data I show how a management idea is constantly shaped and reshaped by fashion setters to ensure its continued viability. From these data, I identify seven distinct response strategies and show how these are associated with the multiple pressures that management consultancies confront, and comprise different implications for the form of an idea. I suggest that this variety of responses is essential to develop a better understanding of the evolution of management ideas because it sheds more light on how and why these commodified forms of management knowledge are reshaped over time, and allows us to better connect population-level life cycle models with firm-level dynamics.

In the next section, I discuss an institutional perspective to study how the contents of a concept might relate only loosely to its label as a response to multiple pressures that confront the management consultants who develop the management idea (Oliver, 1991; Westphal and Zajac, 2001). Then I present the results of the empirical analysis by elaborating on various response strategies consultancies use to deal with the potentially competing pressures to remain legitimate, increase efficiency, and differentiate themselves from competitors, and indicating how these strategies may further understanding about how management knowledge may survive a fashion boom and bust. Finally, I discuss the theoretical implications of the analysis and provide some fruitful directions for further research.

UNDERSTANDING PRESSURES AND RESPONSES

Following the work of Oliver (1991, 1992), who connected the degree of (de)institutionalization to both the strength of pressures exerted on organizations, and the organizations' active agency, various institutional theorists have stressed the importance of studying how organizations satisfy multiple, often competing, pressures (Boxenbaum and Jonsson, 2008; Deephouse, 1999; Greenwood et al., 2010; Pache and Santos, 2010). I first discuss the nature of these pressures and then consider how organizations may respond to them.

Pressures

Institutional theorists suggest that organizations are subject to legitimacy pressures that may enhance or inhibit the institutionalization of particular practices (Oliver, 1991, 1992; Zeitz et al., 1999). These pressures originate from cultural frameworks in the environment (Brunsson and Olsen, 1997; Meyer and Rowan, 1977; Scott, 2001). By conforming to these socially constructed demands (Suchman, 1995), organizations can earn social acceptance among relevant actors in their environment (Scott, 2001; Tolbert and Zucker, 1996). An inability to become socially accepted will likely impede an organization's access to critical resources (Kumar and Das, 2007; Scott, 2001), regardless of their value for the internal functioning of the organization (Staw and Epstein, 2000; Tolbert and Zucker, 1996). These cultural frameworks are crucial for understanding legitimacy pressures on organizations, but scholars also argue that considering only institutional forces is insufficient to explain diversity in organizational responses (e.g. Deephouse, 1999; Kraatz and Zajac, 1996; Oliver, 1992). Rather, legitimacy pressures may interact with efficiency and differentiation pressures.

First, institutional theorists suggest that conformance to legitimacy pressures might contradict efficiency needs (Boxenbaum and Jonsson, 2008; Meyer and Rowan, 1977; Røvik, 1996; Tolbert and Zucker, 1983). Meyer and Rowan (1977: 355) call the adoption of institutional rules from the environment 'pure costs from the point of view of efficiency'. By strictly acceding to legitimacy pressures, the organization limits its internal functioning, because it loses possibilities to optimize its (technical) work activities (Boxenbaum and Jonsson, 2008; Scott, 2001). Second, institutional pressures may also compete with market-related competitive pressures (Deephouse, 1999), in the sense that organizations feel pressured to differentiate themselves from their competitors to improve their competitive positioning, which likely conflicts with the pressure to gain legitimacy (D'Aunno et al., 2000; Delmas and Toffel, 2008; Greenwood and Hinings, 1996; Kraatz and Zajac, 1996). D'Aunno et al. (2000) emphasize the importance of accounting for legitimacy and differentiation pressures together to fully understand the variety of organizational responses in an institutional field.

Responses

Organizations are subject to various pressures, but are not just passive victims of them. Rather, they have some latitude in how they respond to these pressures (Deephouse, 1999; Oliver, 1991; Pache and Santos, 2010; Røvik, 1996), within the specific boundaries that limit which strategic behaviors can take place (Scott, 2001). This latitude exists because of the possibility of decoupling (Brunsson, 1989; Hirsch and Bermiss, 2009; Meyer and Rowan, 1977), in that organizations can avoid pressures by developing different sets of organizational processes for various environments (Fiss and Zajac, 2006; Oliver, 1991; Westphal and Zajac, 2001). In this way, organizations can buffer their work routines from the often-conflicting pressures that stem from intraorganizational dynamics and the organization's environment (Boxenbaum and Jonsson, 2008; Meyer and Rowan, 1977; Oliver, 1992;

Tolbert and Zucker, 1983; Westphal and Zajac, 2001) and thus 'operate independently from these pressures' (Scott, 2001: 173). Decoupling loosens the tensions created as a result of external demands to change and internal preferences to avoid disruptions (Hirsch and Bermiss, 2009; Westphal and Zajac, 2001).

In the context of this research, these perspectives suggest that to understand how management ideas evolve, it is necessary to examine how consultants respond to multiple potentially conflicting pressures. By drawing on these insights from institutional theory, I explore empirically how an idea's interpretive viability offers consultants a range of responses to the pressures they confront when these commodified forms of knowledge appear on the market.

RESPONSE STRATEGIES, PRESSURES, AND IMPLICATIONS

For our data analysis, I concentrated on consultants' perceived pressures and responses in relation to the management idea's evolution, such as changes in the way their firm constructed BPR, to determine how they dealt with the conflicting pressures that arose after the creation and launch of BPR. With our print media, I verified the information collected through the interviews to avoid bias due to retrospective modifications. Three types of pressures emerged from the analysis as crucial elements for the evolving supply-side dynamics of management ideas. Consultants experienced various pressures after they introduced the 'product' on the market: pressures to increase or maintain efficiency and/or legitimacy and/or pressures to differentiate (see Table 7.1). The data also showed that, at several points in time, the consultants perceived these pressures as conflicting, such as when they needed to increase the efficiency of their service but also maintain its legitimacy—that is, simultaneously change and preserve the idea. However, consultants did not simply maintain or abandon their services in the face of these pressures. Rather they drew on a broad range of potential strategies (Table 7.1) to deal with the multiple pressures that they confronted.

On the basis of our analysis, I found that the response strategies could be grouped into three categories: optimization, repositioning, and remarketing. Each category has different implications for the form of a knowledge 'product', in terms of the adaption of the underlying contents, market positioning, and labeling. The following section discusses and illustrates these strategies, how they relate to different pressures, and entail different implications.

Optimization Strategies

The first category of responses emerging from our data involved optimization strategies, that is, a consultancy's strategies to improve the implementation procedure of an existing knowledge 'product' and increase the

Table 7.1 Response strategies, main pressures and implications

Main pressures	Response categories and strategies	Main implications for a concept		
		Δ Contents	Δ Market	Δ Label
Efficiency: high pressure to improve performance during assignments and within firm	**Optimizing:** Enhance efficiency of a concept by improving its underlying contents			
Legitimacy: high pressure to exploit concepts social acceptance	<u>*Streamlining:*</u> Using experiences to smooth the implementation process of a concept	Yes	No	No
Differentiation: low pressure to differentiate	<u>*Standardizing:*</u> Codifying the implementation procedures of a concept to increase possibilities for reuse and leveraging	Yes	No	No
Differentiation: high pressure to be different compared to similar services of competitors and saturation among present clientele	**Repositioning:** Enhance differentiation by developing a specific concept-related market positioning			
	<u>*Refocusing:*</u> Concentrate on a unique interpretation of the concept and present as a specialist in a market niche	No	Yes	No
Efficiency: high pressure to exploit existing expertise	<u>*Broadening:*</u> Expanding a concepts application range by framing it as a solution to a larger number of problem areas	No	Yes	No
Legitimacy: high pressure to exploit social acceptance the concepts has/had in original market	<u>*Relocating:*</u> Introducing the same concept into an entirely different market	No	Yes	No
Legitimacy: high pressure to abandon contaminated label and adopt new or neutral labels	**Remarketing:** Enhance legitimacy of a concept by pre-senting it in a different way on the market			
Efficiency: high pressure to exploit existing expertise	<u>*Relabeling:*</u> Using new/different terms and language for a concept to maintain an image as innovative service supplier	No	No	Yes
Differentiation: low pressure to differentiate	<u>*Normalizing:*</u> Presenting a concept as common part of other services to maintain using underlying contents	No	No	Yes

chances of success for client projects. This response category was used when consultancies felt pressured to enhance the efficiency of the management idea's contents, yet the firm also did not want to jeopardize the legitimacy of the idea. The data revealed that efficiency pressures originated when consultants experienced inadequate performance in their use of the 'product' in client assignments. Optimization offered the possibility of enhancing efficiency by adapting the extant contents, without harming the legitimacy of the overall practice. The data revealed two distinct strategies in relation to this response category.

Strategy 1: Streamlining
To respond to pressures to increase the technical performance of the knowledge 'product' and related practice while maintaining legitimacy, firms streamline the contents underlying the idea. For example, informants experienced that if a BPR implementation took too long or ran into complications, it lessened client satisfaction and ultimately undermined the consultancy's and management idea's reputation. Therefore, several consultants indicated that they learned from previous experiences to smooth out the methods and implementation procedures associated with BPR. By adapting BPR's underlying contents, they worked to deploy it more efficiently and reduced the resources needed to execute a related project.

The changes to the management idea's contents were not accompanied by modifications to the marketing of the idea. The consultants' services were still sold under a popular banner, so consultants could improve the functioning of their methods (and increase efficiency) while still drawing on and maintaining legitimacy (to generate new sales). One managing consultant stressed this strategy by describing:

> Those adaptations [to the BPR concept] were particularly the result of our experiences at [consultancy M]. We saw that some of our BPR trajectories simply lasted too long [. . .]. We used to pay a lot of attention to the analysis of the current situation by exploring the functioning of the organization. In those trajectories we made an advanced design, but that was soon outdated because of the developments in the environment. That's why we try to keep the analysis phase [of the new BPR trajectories] as brief as possible. (V3)

In the media publications (e.g. B2a, F2a, D1b, and P4b), I found various instances of consultants adapting the contents of a 'product' through streamlining. For example, one consultant initially wrote about BPR's contents in terms of 'radically approaching the primary processes and redesign them with IT as a leverage' (Q2a, p. 7), and then just two years later, adapted his initial interpretation to promote a cyclical, step-by-step approach and warn, 'the reengineering thinking of the last couple of years is dangerous because the implementation is too complex and takes too long' (Q2d, p. 66). The same idea was being marketed, but consultants reinterpreted it and made inconspicuous changes to its contents. In his interview, the same consultant confirmed that even while using the same label, his interpretation of the idea had changed significantly over time:

> My lesson from the experiences with BPR was that often you cannot do it all at once, but have to manage it in cycles of change. With this you could say that I more or less abandoned the initial BPR philosophy. (Q2)

Strategy 2: Standardizing

Another response involved standardizing a knowledge product's underlying contents without changing anything in formal communications to the market. Standardization entails codifying the management idea's contents in more detail and internally disseminating it to further a shared understanding of 'how to do BPR' among consultants within a firm. For example, attempts to routinize the various elements of BPR included standard frameworks and implementation methods. Although the idea's content changes, it is regarded mainly as an internal issue, without consequences for its labeling in the market. Standardization may enhance efficiency by allowing consultants to reuse material from prior assignments, as I observed in several articles (D1a, V2c, P4a, Q2a, T1a, T1b, and T2a).

Standardization was particularly used when consultants felt pressured to become more efficient in the commercialization and implementation of a particular management idea; they continued to draw on and feed the initial legitimacy of the idea while routinizing the generation of assignments and service delivery. Our informants indicated that standardizing may improve communication, both among consultants and with customers, which also increases the efficiency of idea deployment. Standardized language, methods, and models facilitate intraorganizational learning and make it easier to assign inexperienced (i.e. less expensive) consultants to BPR projects. Legitimacy remains though, because the BPR banner still flies. Standardizing could even increase a management idea's legitimacy as a general framework, and a common language used by all consultants may give clients a better impression of BPR's value. For example, a director of a consultancy described how consultants seek to standardize an idea's contents to improve the impression they give to possible clients:

> The initial concept remained standing, but it has been detailed into methods, techniques, and tools. Initially we came to the client with just a number of vague PowerPoint slides [. . .]. But when BPR became more commoditized, and also was adopted by other consultancies, we had to be better documented and build up a better experience database. For

instance, currently we have elaborate databases of every sector and industry you can imagine, including various improvements that have been applied in these projects. (Q1)

Repositioning Strategies

A second category of responses that arose from the data is repositioning. This refers to a firm's strategies focused on adapting the position of the knowledge product in the market in comparison with potential competitors. The content and the label remained the same, but consultants tried to sell it to another market or market segment. These strategies arose mainly when consultancies perceived limited possibilities to differentiate their product-related service offerings from those of competitors, even though they still wanted to use the idea's legitimacy in the field and maintain efficiency by drawing on their concept-related experience. I discovered three distinct repositioning strategies.

Strategy 1: Refocusing

A first strategy that could be discerned concerns narrowing the knowledge commodity's interpretation to focus on specialist market niches. When competitors entered the market with their own version of BPR, it was seen as an important incentive to achieve a clearer position as a specialist for a particular aspect of this idea. As they remained active in the same market and used the same contents and (legitimate) labels, these firms tried to differentiate from (new) competitors by focusing on specific, narrower types of BPR assignments, thereby associating themselves with a particular niche in the BPR market.

I found a number of different instances of refocusing in the data, such as N2a (HRM-focused approach), and U1a (organizational structural approach). Some firms targeted clients particularly interested in more formalized approaches to BPR (B2a, B4a, and F2a); others focused on a strategic business transformation view of BPR to distinguish themselves from more IT-focused competitors offering BPR services (Q2c). The director of a consultancy thus explained how his firm sought to adapt its market position to address pressures to differentiate while retaining the use of the same label and practices:

> Some years after our first BPR projects, IT consultancies started to embrace the concept [. . .]. We concluded that those consultancies only were involved in process reengineering and strongly associated this with IT. We positioned ourselves with a much more strategic approach [to BPR]. We were particularly equipped for designing and guiding transformations of two to three years, and we still approach it that way

[. . .]. This was positioned as something substantially different than those [consultancies who offered] process redesign trajectories. (P4)

Still other informants indicated that they sought to refocus by 'upgrading' their BPR approach to a more strategic level and concentrate on more firm-wide, general, and long-term applications. In such a case the same 'product' (BPR) is used, but repositioned as a large-scale strategic effort. Such a response strategy allows consultancies to make their 'products' more distinct and maintain the efficiency of their previous investments in the idea. At the same time, it also allows for the possibility of retaining the label under which the service is presented to the market, thereby still drawing on the management idea's legitimacy. For instance, one senior consultant explained that they still used the label BPR, but reserved it for more strategy-level assignments, in the expectation that this specific market niche would generate more revenues:

> So the consulting division of firm [K] considered the BPR concept as an important means to become more 'up-market', create more added value, and perform bigger projects. So they just wanted to have the strategic mega projects and compete with consultancies such as Booz Allen Hamilton, BCG, and McKinsey. (K3)

Strategy 2: Broadening
In contrast, while the previous strategy aims at limiting the idea's interpretation, a second response strategy that emerges from the data involves broadening the application range of BPR, that is, positioning their BPR services as more inclusive. Once established, consultants may experience the clients' problem situation in which they applied BPR as being too narrow to take full advantage of their expertise. Associating the same underlying contents of this commodified form of knowledge to a broader variety of client problems allows consultants to differentiate their expertise, but still draw on and feed the label's legitimacy. By widening the application range, consultants could present themselves as generalists, thereby enhancing the likelihood to generate more assignments and selling their expertise, using the same management idea.

I found examples of this response strategy in various instances (K1b, P4c, Q1a, Q2e, Q2f, Q2g, V2b, and V2c). For example, a consultant stressed that BPR should go beyond a single focus on cost cutting: 'The real BPR is a means to improve the internal and external power of an organization. Not only cost reduction' (P4c, p. 356). An author emphasized in his article on 'second-generation BPR' that 'future BPR will increasingly focus on more difficult processes such as sales processes within an organization (V2c, p. 16). In other words, the well-known BPR label was associated with adjacent domains. In our interview with this consultant, he explained that he sought to relate BPR to an increasing number of different organizational problems that might be considered relevant by his potential clientele, thereby finding a source of new assignments for his expertise:

> We have increasingly used [BPR] for less obvious processes. So now we apply it not only to back-office processes at administrative offices, but also at front offices, multichannel, and professional services. (V2)

Broadening is seen as an important means to enhance differentiation while retaining the management idea's underlying contents and label for presenting the service to the market. Extending the range of problems and solutions ultimately related to trajectories that generated more revenues. Thus the board of directors of one consultancy decided to refocus the BPR 'product' by associating it also with IT-related issues such as SAP implementations. This form of repositioning aimed to enhance the consultancy's business by being more inclusive, in that:

> Using BPR as front stage for SAP implementation worked out quite well in terms of revenues. As a result, at a certain moment most BPR projects led to SAP implementations. (T2)

Strategy 3: Relocating

A final strategy related to repositioning involves locating the same knowledge 'product' in an entirely different market sector. I found that this strategy was especially favored when consultants promoted their management idea in a saturated market, making it difficult to differentiate themselves. Moving to an entirely different market with few competitors active with BPR and where BPR was still uncontroversial offered an appropriate strategy in these circumstances. For example, in the print media publications, I found examples of consultancies that tried to relocate the BPR 'product' to the banking and insurance (W1a) or health care (K4a, K4b, V3a) sectors. One informant recalled that his consultancy found it increasingly difficult to stand out from the crowd, so it looked to other markets to sell its BPR expertise and found the health care sector very receptive:

> BPR is becoming more and more accepted in health care. This becomes apparent gradually, but very explicitly in the number of assignments that is starting to develop. Also in the newspapers you can read more and more about the problems in the health care sector. At the same time, money seems to be less a problem given that the government sees ICT as a central issue within health care to invest in [. . .]. Therefore, to do BPR assignments in this sector, we asked some people within [consultancy K] who had a lot of experience in BPR projects to provide a specific education program for our Health care Group

[. . .]. The concept has become an important and promising product because we feel that the health care sector is becoming more open to this concept. (K4)

With relocating, the consultancy would use the legitimacy the management idea gained in other markets and exploit its expertise with implementing it. For example, when entering the health care sector, some BPR consultancies explicitly noted that BPR had been used successfully in other sectors. Although it provides new opportunities to maintain an idea's underlying contents and draws on a label's legitimacy, relocating existing commodified forms of knowledge into a new market is considered not unproblematic; it requires the consultancy to obtain an in-depth understanding of the next market to be able to contextualize the idea appropriately. Thus the marketing approach should be positioned to fit the specific language and problems of a new group of clients. One informant described his firm's relocating effort as follows:

While in other branches we were already beyond the hype, for commercial reasons we thought it was clever to maintain calling our approach BPR in the health care sector. We started propagating the notion of BPR in the health care sector and emphasized that we know a lot about this concept through our prior experiences in other sectors. However, initially [consultancy M] was not able to exploit this market themselves because they did not have the right networks and did not speak its language. Therefore, I was hired to further develop this market. (V3)

Remarketing Strategies

A final response category that I found in our data was remarketing, referring to a firm's strategies that focus on naming an established management idea in a different way, but changing little of its actual contents or market positioning. Our analysis reveals that remarketing strategies are appropriate when consultants experience strong legitimacy pressures to abandon the knowledge 'product', but want to remain efficient by continuing to use the same underlying contents. For example, our informants indicate that, at a certain point, BPR had become contaminated and considered 'no longer fashionable' (P1), 'less popular' (C2), 'yesterday's thing' (Q1), or even an 'obsolete product' (P4) that 'can no longer be sold' (B1). Presenting the knowledge 'product' in a different way offered a productive strategy for addressing this tension. Our analysis revealed two remarketing strategies.

Strategy 1: Relabeling
Consultants indicated that when a 'new' competing management idea acquires prominent status in the managerial discourse, they feel pressured to

adopt the new terms, labels, and language associated with this new idea to convey the impression that they (and their services) remain state-of-the-art. The interpretive space of the idea allows these consultants to offer similar service components and draw on established knowledge and experiences, under the banner of different, uncontaminated terms. I found this strategy in various cases in the investigated articles: The term BPR had been replaced by labels such as business process management (BPM) (B2c, C1a, D1c, I1b), E-business (D1d, Q1c), straight through processing (STP) (I1c, I1d), knowledge management (K3d), and outsourcing (Q1d). Our data suggested that consultancies used these new labels for the same BPR services to address the declining legitimacy of the term while preserving the efficiency of the underlying contents. A striking example came from a managing consultant who emphasized that, to enhance the legitimacy of his service, he increasingly presented it with a new label:

> Every client that called only wanted to hear E-something. And of course, as a consultancy you will sell E-everything. We totally abandoned the term BPR because that was out of fashion. I used the same slides, only then under the label of E-Business [. . .]. It's striking when you consider E-Business, you'll find all business processes again: production, logistics, procurement, marketing, and sales. That's not new. It's all BPR. (T2)

A variation on this strategy involved not just using newer and more fashionable terms, but reframing client questions in neutral terms to fit the firm's existing services. Our informants indicated that whenever BPR developed a pejorative connotation among clients, they just stopped mentioning the label. The client's request was reformulated using less controversial terms to describe the consultancy's established BPR concept. That is, the knowledge commodity's name was avoided in communications between the consultant and the client, but the consultant offered the same service and presented it as useful. As one informant noted:

> For us as consultants the term BPR neither has a positive or a negative connotation. But clients may be hesitant because they associate it with large-scale changes. So as a consultant you just name it differently, but do the same. (Q1)

Strategy 2: Normalizing
Portraying an established management idea as a normal element of new service offerings constituted a second remarketing strategy. An unfavorable connotation of the BPR 'product' in the external environment made selling services under the BPR label difficult for consultants. When consultants noticed that its legitimacy was decreasing, some of them presented their BPR service explicitly as a useful part of other services. In my print media data

(Appendix II), I found several instances in which consultants explicitly pre-sented BPR as common practice in workflow management (B2b, B5a, and I1a), organizational change trajectories (J1a), data warehousing (J1b), and balanced scorecard (BSC) approaches (Q1b).

One telling example came from a consultant who authored an article on BPR during the 1990s and two articles in 2001 on straight through process-ing (STP), which aimed to propagate the improvement of work processes among actors. The resemblance between his BPR and STP articles was striking. In both articles, workflow appeared as a key element in a success-ful organizational change project (I1a, p. 57; I1c, p. 10). That is, existing competencies related to workflow, which originated in BPR, continued to be presented as part of a consultancy's service, but now as an essential ele-ment of a new form of commodified knowledge. Consultants from other firms similarly framed the idea as a conventional part of a broader approach when the BPR label was contaminated:

> I no longer use the term [BPR] so often, even though I do the same kind of projects. Every time I do the Redesign workshop for a client, I explic-itly tell the client that BPR has been developed in the early 1990s as a philosophy so they know that they are applying the BPR concept. But that does not mean that the entire project is labeled BPR. Rather, the practice is presented as, for example, improving work processes. (N2)

CONCLUSION

Using an institutional perspective, this chapter has explored how consultan-cies respond to competing pressures after a knowledge commodity has been established, and sheds more light on how management ideas may remain viable, even after their popularity declines. By identifying seven response strategies and showing how these are associated with multiple pressures, and comprise different implications for the form of a commodity, the present chapter develops a more fluid conceptualization of the evolving supply-side dynamics of commodified forms of management knowledge. These find-ings pushes the study of management knowledge commodification beyond the assumption that knowledge entrepreneurs simply abandon or maintain their 'products' as a response to changes in their legitimacy. In addition they indicate that the continuous shaping and reshaping of management ideas is essential to 'stretch' their lives and increase the likelihood that management knowledge survives a collapse in popularity.

Thus whereas prior literature primarily views the evolving supply-side dynamics of management ideas as homogeneous and predetermined, the analysis in this chapter indicates[1] three response categories, comprising seven response strategies, which management consultants adopt to deal with multiple pressures. A first category of response strategies was associated with consultancies that felt pressured to enhance the efficiency of the idea, yet also did not want to jeopardize its legitimacy. Such efficiency pressures may originate from consultants who experienced inadequate performance in their use of the management idea in client assignments. This chapter discussed two distinct optimization strategies in relation to this response category, that is streamlining and standardizing, each associated with adaptations to the contents of the management knowledge 'product' without changing its marketing or labeling.

A second category of responses that was discussed in this chapter refers to consultancy's strategies focused on adapting the position of the management idea in the market in comparison with potential competitors while leaving its contents and labeling unchanged. These repositioning strategies— refocusing, broadening, and relocating—arose mainly when consultancies perceived limited possibilities to differentiate their management idea-related service offerings from those of competitors, even though they still wanted to use the idea's legitimacy in the field and maintain efficiency by drawing on their related experience.

The third response category that I discussed in this chapter refers to a consultancy's strategies that focus on adapting the naming of an established management idea, but changing little of its actual contents or market positioning. I elaborated on two remarketing strategies, relabeling and normalizing, each related to consultants who experience strong legitimacy pressures to abandon their knowledge 'product', but want to remain efficient by continuing to use the same underlying contents and focusing on similar groups of potential clients. Presenting the idea in a different way offered a productive strategy for addressing this tension.

8 Conclusion

I started this book with the question: where do management ideas come from? In the first chapter I have argued that this is a nontrivial question given that many of these ideas have been established in the canon of management while the social practices that have produced these ideas remain largely hidden (see also Shenhav, 1999). In order to address this central question I drew from the literature on commodification because it preludes prior discussions on management idea production and allows shedding more light on its social life or cultural biography, an issue that received scant attention in the literature about the supply-side dynamics of management ideas. This allowed developing a broader, processual conceptualization of commodification in which commodities are not solely considered in economic terms, but as 'things' of which their exchangeability is a socially relevant element in the past, present, or future (Appadurai, 1986; 2005), and commodification 'is best looked upon as a process of becoming rather than as an all-or-none state of being' (Kopytoff, 1986: 73). This entails that commodified forms of management knowledge are hypothesized as having their own 'biography', and studying these knowledge commodities goes beyond solely focusing on the moment or state of an idea's exchange, taking into account their total trajectory from initial conception through development, maturity, and decline. In line with this framework, I sought to empirically trace 'new' management ideas and practices back to their fabrication in the context of management consultancies. As Sturdy et al. argued: '. . . further insight in the role of consultancy in the development of new management practices could be achieved by extending research back into early product development' (2009: 177). In the context of this research, this perspective allowed to develop a better understanding about the way consultants as central knowledge entrepreneurs construct commodified forms of knowledge throughout different stages in their social life.

In seeking to further uncover the 'social life' of commodified forms of management knowledge, the book provides five empirical chapters, each drawing on distinct theoretical backdrops that stem from market orientation literature, product innovation literature, practice-based perspectives, and institutional theory. While these theoretical backdrops may differ significantly in their key foci and underlying assumptions, collectively the chapters follow along the lines of a cultural biography, that is, the way relevant social groups construct a management idea's social life from initial conception to adolescence, maturity, and decline. After providing an overview of three different streams of research in the prior literature on the production of management ideas in chapter 2, chapter 3 focuses on the ostensibly initial stages in the life history of an idea by exploring the way management consultants sense 'incipient preferences' among their clients. In particular it reveals how management consultants acquire, interpret, and utilize client information and how this is translated into 'new' commodities. Chapters 4 and 5 then move the focus from market orientation to primarily relevant intraorganizational dimensions. In particular chapter 4 identifies a number of key activities through which a commodity may proceed within a consultancy, and explains how these firms deal with the conflicting demands that inevitably accompany such innovation processes. Relatedly, chapter 5 provides an understanding of the internal impediments to the establishment of 'new' knowledge commodities within consultancies and shows the importance of gaining legitimacy for these commodified forms of management knowledge among peers. Subsequently, chapter 6 moves the focus again to relevant external dimensions by exploring the way management consultants construct commodified forms of knowledge as enacted practice. In particular it identifies key framing moves that consultants draw upon to make sense of and justify possible translations of these ideas in relation to a client situation. Finally, chapter 7 discusses how supply-side dynamics shape the way management ideas evolve and how management knowledge may survive a fashion boom and bust. It identifies several relevant response strategies employed by consultants and show how these are associated with multiple pressures and comprises different implications for an idea's evolution.

In the remainder of this concluding chapter I seek to synthesize the findings from the different analyses by elaborating on how each chapter (1) can contribute to our understanding of the way innovation and commodification takes shape in management consultancies, (2) can shed further light on the development and evolution of management ideas, and the production of cultural artifacts more generally, and (3) can contribute to critical reflections on the treatise of taken-for-granted and influential ideas in the world of management. Following Appadurai's conceptualization of the study of commodities as 'things' that 'at a certain phase in their careers and in a particular context, meet the requirements of commodity candidacy' (1986: 16) the insights offered in these preceding chapters to our understanding of the evolving supply-side dynamics of commodified forms of management knowledge comes together in the intersection between three key dimensions (see Table 8.1).

PATHS AND DIVERSIONS

One important implication that can be derived from the discussions in the five empirical chapters relates to conceptualizing management knowledge commodification as comprising different routes. This is in line with

Table 8.1 Key dimensions in the social life of management ideas

Sensing (CH 3)	Tensions (CH 4)	Currency (CH 5)	Practice (CH 6)	Cycles (CH 7)
Paths and diversions				
Iterations between internal and external dimensions	Diversity in how commodification activities are performed	Commodities are not necessarily fully developed	Commodities viewed as more or less open-ended practice	Distinct elements of commodity may follow divergent trajectories
Drivers and impediments				
External and internal legitimacy	Organization-structural arrangements and commodification routines	Barriers to gaining internal legitimacy stemming from lack of fit and lack of involvement	Limitations to possibilities of alternative translation reflecting local situation, past socializations, and firm routines	Commodities constantly under efficiency, legitimacy, and differentiation pressures
Spheres and agency				
Performance of organizational capabilities that enable learning from clients	Compensating mechanism that enhance focus or entrepreneurship	Presence and abilities of product champion	Translation shaped by framing moves related to dispositional and interactive-situational dimensions	Evolution not predetermined, but shaped by different response strategies

Appadurai's understanding that considers the flow of commodities in any given situation as 'a shifting compromise between socially regulated paths and competitively inspired diversions' (1986: 17). While much of prior literature presents the development of successful commodities as a series of logical and straightforward phases unavoidably resulting in a knowledge product that can be immediately sold on the market for managerial solutions, the analysis in this book indicated that there is a need to place greater emphasis on the diversions.

First, in chapter 4 we saw that although commodification efforts may share some general activities, the way these activities are carried out varies considerably between different firms. As Cooper (1983, 12) already noted, development trajectories of 'novel' ideas display important differences; and in this study we demonstrated that consultancies may diverge between professional-driven and corporate-driven forms, each with its own specific tensions and difficulties. The findings also revealed important differences in the way consultancies seek to stimulate commodification ventures either by creating focus or by enhancing entrepreneurship. In addition, the discussion in chapter 5 indicates that prior literature tends to focus primarily on ex-post successful commodities. However, by focusing on the time commodities were constructed, the chapter revealed how new management ideas are not necessarily considered self-evident or perceived as beneficial, thereby suggesting that there is also significant variety to the extent commodification processes are completed and new ideas are actually established within a knowledge entrepreneur (see also van de Ven, 1986; Anand et al., 2007). Hence, overall, this study reflects the need to devote more research attention to the factors that may explain the variety of different ways processes of commodification are performed.

Second, the analyses in this book, and particularly in chapter 7, reveals that commodified forms of management knowledge are understood as comprising different elements which are systematically associated with divergent evolution patterns. Specifically, by showing that knowledge 'products' continuously undergo changes to their (1) contents, (2) market positioning, or (3) labeling, the present study highlights the significance of (de)coupling as a key mechanism for understanding the evolving supply of management ideas. While Czarniawska and Sevón (1996) refer to the translation of ideas as an ongoing dynamic process, prior analyses of supply-side dynamics focus on the evolution of a single label (Abrahamson, 1996; Abrahamson and Fairchild, 1999; David and Strang, 2006) and treat management ideas as stable products, primarily modified during their implementation (Ansari et al., 2010; Benders and Verlaar, 2003; Frenkel, 2005), without specifying alternative ways in which these knowledge entrepreneurs persistently couple and decouple different elements of these ideas to enhance the longevity of their expertise. This entails that knowledge commodities do not necessarily follow a single, predetermined evolution pattern and that management consultants' strategies constitute an important basis for different evolution trajectories.

Such a fluid, dynamic conceptualization of the evolving supply-side dynamics also suggests more gradual changes in the evolution of organizational knowledge than the rapid and ostensibly revolutionary turnover in management ideas would suggest (Jacques, 1996; Lammers, 1988; Perkmann and Spicer, 2008). Rather, our study explains that given the possibility of (de)coupling among a management idea's contents, market positioning, and labeling, factors that may enhance or inhibit the idea's longevity cannot relate to just a single entity uniform pattern of development, but should be understood in terms of a diversity of related trajectories (Oliver, 1992; Perkmann and Spicer, 2008; Zeitz et al., 1999). This would imply that future intraorganizational analyses of the evolution of fashionable ideas should not only account for different forces that may enhance or inhibit institutionalization of ideas, but also account for a constellation of different context-specific sedimentations, each with its own possible development route.

DRIVERS AND IMPEDIMENTS

Another fruitful corollary from the preceding chapters relates to the importance of understanding the different elements that drive and impede processes of commodification. An underlying assumption that pertains to prior conceptualizations is that commodification processes are mainly driven by cues to externally legitimate a commodity's exchange value and that internally these processes largely proceed as harmonious, thereby automatically enjoying the assistance and support of many other people within a consultancy. An important limitation in the current research is that there is still little attention to the underlying and often competing drivers that define and impede the possible exchangeability of management ideas in a particular sociotemporal context.

First, the various analyses in this book indicate that knowledge commodification is not solely a matter of constructing a coherent 'product' and subsequently attempting to externally legitimate its exchange value in the market. Rather, a more fundamental problem lies in making a new management idea become established in a consultancy and gain internal legitimacy before or during market launch. Particularly chapter 3 and chapter 5 show that commodification efforts do not necessarily fit with established practices and do not habitually meet with a favorable response within consultancies. The findings showed that consultants perceive major impediments in linking a new idea to their organizational strategy and resources. Indeed, the knowledge-intensive character of consultancies and their ideational 'products' imply that the establishment of new management ideas within consultancies entails drawing on political and persuasive skills in order to seduce organizational members to support new ideas. As Alvesson argues, 'The ambiguities involved in work and results mean that *internally* as well as *externally* great efforts must be made in order to emphasize [. . .] that experts should be relied upon' (1993: 1011, emphases added). This reveals a need for more research to understand the sociopolitical process in which new management ideas gain 'good currency' (van de Ven, 1986) within knowledge entrepreneurs.

Second, by showing that the evolving supply-side dynamics are continuously influenced by multiple and potentially competing pressures, we provide a deeper, more nuanced understanding of the underlying rationales as to why these management ideas are reshaped over time. Prior studies focus primarily on the legitimacy of a knowledge 'product' as the key element driving its supply-side dynamics (Abrahamson, 1996; Abrahamson and Fairchild, 1999; David and Strang, 2006; Kieser, 1997). In chapter 7 this study points out that management consultants not only take legitimacy pressures into account in processes of knowledge commodification, but also consider efficiency and differentiation pressures as relevant. In other words, the tension among pressures of legitimacy, efficiency, and differentiation drives supply-side changes in the content, the positioning, or the labeling, and thus ultimately shapes the evolution of a management idea. Our findings also indicate that pressures experienced by knowledge entrepreneurs to change management ideas are not limited to one time period; rather, ideas remain continuously 'under pressure' after they emerge on the market. This resonates with Czarniawska and Sevón's (1996) work that refers to translation as a dynamic process in knowledge transfer, but this book extends this by elucidating the main drivers of translation and indicating that the relative strength of these drivers vary over time. For instance, chapter 7 indicated that while a management idea is popular, it likely seems legitimate, but still comes under increased pressure for being less efficient or offering only limited possibilities for differentiation. Later, the idea's legitimacy could come under more pressure, but the relative strength of differentiation pressures may be relatively lower. Regardless of the case, getting a better understanding of multiple pressures is important, because it provides a more nuanced picture of the drivers of supply-side dynamics that shape the evolving translation of management ideas and sheds further light on the reasons knowledge entrepreneurs respond as they do.

SOCIAL SPHERES AND AGENCY

A third implication relates to the crucial role of human agency not only in legitimizing commodified forms of management knowledge, but also in constantly shaping and reshaping these ideas during the different stages in their social life to enhance and maintain exchange value throughout different social spheres. In explaining the social life of a commodity, the work of Appadurai stresses the significance of linking 'the social environment of the commodity and its temporal and symbolic state' (1986: 15). Indeed, despite that a growing body of literature has pointed to the interactive nature of processes through which management ideas are 'constructed, reconstructed, negotiated and substituted in a dialectic between consultant and client . . .' (Sturdy, 1997: 408; see also Clark and Salaman, 1998; Reihlen and Nikolova, 2010), existing analyses of supply-side dynamics have paid scant attention to how this exactly takes shape. To address this issue, this book sheds further light on the way knowledge entrepreneurs construct and reconstruct management ideas in relation to different sociotemporal contexts such as the broader management knowledge market or the specific consultant-client relationship.

First, the findings in chapters 3 and 5 showed how consultants seek to 'orchestrate' the interaction between external and internal dimensions in relation to the development of a marketable and saleable management idea. Previous work stresses that the client plays an important role in the production of new management ideas in consultancies (Clark and Greatbatch, 2004; Fosstenløkken et al., 2003) and points to the importance of 'sensing incipient preferences' (Abrahamson, 1996; Suddaby and Greenwood, 2001). This would imply that a 'good nose' for new marketable products is a vital element at the start of a commodification venture. This book extends this argument by showing the importance of market sensing throughout the whole project of commodification in consultancies. In chapter 3 it is argued that the development of new commodified forms of knowledge is systematically associated with constantly staying in tune with the market. Initially, this involves checking the marketability of a management idea in an embryonic state. When this becomes more concrete over time, market checks remain necessary in various ways. These checks are not only needed to deliver a marketable product, but also to persuade internal stakeholders such as the management and a consultant's peers to go along with the novel idea-in-development.

Thus the present study reveals the necessity to further the analysis into how client needs play a role in innovation processes and how this is considered crucial to the success of a new knowledge product. These issues receive increasing attention but are still underdeveloped in the current research on the supply of management ideas. As Anand et al. have stated: 'innovation in knowledge-based organizations is particularly challenging owing to the ambiguous nature of knowledge itself' (2007: 406). Indeed, while market information and clients' responses are considered vital input for commodification ventures (e.g. Clark and Greatbatch, 2004), this is considered inherently ambiguous and subject to change, which likely feeds different opinions and controversies during its interpretation and enactment of market information (see Daft and Weick, 1984). Therefore, more research is needed not only to uncover the antecedents and consequences of market orientation in management knowledge commodification, but also to develop a better understanding of organizational learning barriers that may influence the acquisition, internal dissemination, and use of relevant market information in relation to the production of management ideas.

Second, there is the issue of how the application of new management ideas takes shape within client organizations. This is a highly relevant issue because the development of management ideas is never fully completed, but involves ongoing activity because these 'products' cannot be easily separated from the specific consultant who is producing and applying these commodified forms of knowledge (Clark, 1995). As Morris noted about consultants, 'a core of their work concerned interpretation' (Morris, 2001: 835). The framing moves that we identified in chapter 6 not only help clarify relevant processes and tensions inherent to management knowledge commodification, but also point to important limitations to possibilities of translation, a significant, albeit largely unexplored, phase in relation to the commodification of management knowledge (Benders and van Veen, 2001; Clark, 2004; Suddaby and Greenwood, 2001). Indeed, in line with the seminal work of Czarniawska and Sevón (1996), Suddaby and Greenwood (2001: 939) conceptualize this phase as 're-application of codified and abstracted knowledge into a variety of different organizational contexts' (see also Mueller and Whittle, 2011), however, rather than regard consultants as highly flexible or pragmatic in 'translating' management ideas to a specific problem situation (Benders et al., 1998; Benders and van Veen, 2001; Morris, 2001; Werr et al., 1997) the analyses revealed that consultants perceived major impediments to their ability to regard management ideas as open-ended per se or automatically agreed with any client interpretation. Such limitations to framing concepts as open-ended practice reflect not only the local situation, but also the consultants' past socializations and the broader firm routines in which they are embedded. These processes imply important preconditions that might significantly reduce alternative interpretations and uses of ideas during the implementation stage, an issue that has received scant attention in prior research. Thus identifying key framing moves may help explain why the translation of a management idea by consultants does not always feature unlimited variation in the possible interpretations; it also clarifies why consultants cannot be understood solely as pragmatic in their enactment of management ideas.

The discussion above has indicated that a fruitful avenue for future research would be to pay more attention to how management consultancies deal with management ideas during their assignments, and what factors and conditions play a role in the consumption of these ideas (Strang, 2010; Heusinkveld et al., 2011). This would allow further strengthening of the link between supply- and demand-related approaches to studying management ideas, streams of research that have remained relatively separate in the prior literature. Relatedly, considering the heterogeneity in consultants' backgrounds and strategic positions (Visscher, 2006), as well as the low entry barriers for this industry (Clark, 1995), research should further examine how consultants' conceptual repertoires relate to their approaches to address organizational problems and how these affect consultants' use of management knowledge commodities. Such an investigation could offer a better understanding of the variety of firms that provide the 'bewildering range of services' (Clark and Fincham, 2002: 4) and how this may pose limitations to possible translations of management ideas.

Third, by identifying various response strategies in chapter 7, the book indicates the importance of studying knowledge entrepreneurs' agency to better understand a knowledge commodity's social life. Most conceptualizations in prior literature view evolving supply-side dynamics of management ideas as homogeneous and predetermined (Abrahamson and Fairchild, 1999; Gill and Whittle, 1993; Giroux, 2006; Huczynski, 1993), but the analyses in chapter 7 indicate the significance of knowledge entrepreneurs' agency by identifying three response categories, comprising seven response strategies, which management consultants adopt to deal with multiple pressures. This important finding pushes the study of management knowledge commodification beyond the assumption that knowledge entrepreneurs simply abandon or maintain their knowledge 'products' (e.g. Abrahamson and Fairchild, 1999; David and Strang, 2006; Huczynski, 1993). In addition, the research reveals that managerial consultants have a much broader variety of options at their disposal to 'stretch' a commodity's longevity. All these strategies should be recognized as significant for developing a more open-ended, agency-driven comprehension of the supply-side dynamics of management ideas (see also Whittle, 2008).

An open-ended, agency-driven understanding of a management idea's evolution does not preclude the general tendency by which optimization strategies are more likely during an upswing phase, repositioning strategies become most conspicuous later in the cycle, and remarketing strategies are likely to emerge in the downswing. Rather the findings show that each consultancy may experience a specific (likely shifting) mix of pressures that stem from its environment or intraorganizational dynamics, which shape its response at any particular point in time. This agency-driven conceptualization also offers a better understanding of the variations in management knowledge commodities' life cycles by relating consultancies' strategic decisions to the potential to extend an idea's longevity. Specifically, our study implies that continuity, or 'old wine in new bottles', is not a given, but rather relates to firms' strategies and in particular their responses to efficiency pressures. Similarly, it also allows for better understanding whether and why experience with applying management ideas, even outdated ones, does not necessarily disappear into oblivion. Rather, these ideas can be retained and reapplied to new commodified forms of management knowledge because they may not be put 'under pressure'.

In its identification of possibilities for agency, this study offers an exploratory first step toward developing a more fine-grained understanding of the evolution of commodified forms of management knowledge. It should be complemented by other studies that address remaining questions in this research area. For instance, additional studies might provide more clarity regarding the antecedents and consequences of the identified alternative strategies. Moreover, following Fligstein (1997), the social skills of knowledge entrepreneurs include the ability to identify the interest of relevant actors within a specific field, and using this as a basis for 'strategic action' (1997: 398) that convinces others of the value of new management ideas. This may point to the need for further understanding about how knowledge entrepreneurs make sense of the pressures that confront them, and how they deal with them by creatively seeking to capitalize on the opportunities they find, developing and justifying combinations of new and familiar avenues and monitoring the reactions of other stakeholders (especially clients) before pursuing a new strategy (cf. Cornelissen and Clarke, 2010). In addition, research should shed more light on important intraorganizational forces that determine the longevity of management knowledge in consulting practice. This could shed more light on how and to what extent 'old' ideas appear in new management knowledge production cycles (Suddaby and Greenwood, 2001). The presence of elements from previous management ideas is no guarantee that related expertise can be reused and entrenched (Zeitz et al., 1999) or that consultants might not reinvent the wheel.

ALIENATION AND ACCUMULATION

As argued above, to further insight into the supply-side dynamics of management ideas there is a need to look beyond the 'commodity situation'. In line with Ertman and Williams (2005), this book does not seek to engage in debates for or against commodified forms of knowledge, while at the same time not denying the significant value of these debates. Indeed, these debates have generated important insights that have been helpful in understanding how commodification can be seen as an inextricable element of contemporary capitalist societies and in developing a critical view that recognizes the possibilities and limitations of interpreting people, objects, and ideas in terms of (quasi)exchange value. Rather, drawing on a cultural perspective, I seek to show how widely known and taken-for-granted ideas in the world of management can be seen as the result of different collective social processes of productivization or commodification (see also Becker, 1974; Peterson, 1979) that comprise different routes, are propelled by various and sometimes competing key drivers, and occur in distinct social environments. This entails that commodified forms of knowledge currently included in many standard textbooks on management and regarded as an established element of the accepted management vocabulary were not so self-evident or widely perceived as valuable during the time they were initially constructed and marketed. Therefore, by considering a knowledge commodity's 'social life' (Appadurai, 1986; Kopytoff, 1986), this book seeks to emphasize for students of management and organization, as well as management practitioners, the significance of studying and scrutinizing processes of management ideas' fabrication including the underlying interests, intentions, beliefs, and values of those that produce them.

Studying a management idea's social life may not only allow a better understanding of the inherent ambivalence towards commodified forms of management knowledge, but also contribute to recognizing how commodified management knowledge may easily alienate students of management from the social processes that shape the way influential ideas are fabricated, thereby creating a potential misleading impression of management ideas as objective, ahistorical, and universal (see also Jacques, 1996; Shenhav, 1999; ten Bos, 2000; Suddaby and Greenwood, 2001). Moreover, this book also seeks to stress the importance of understanding the difficulties in studying the social life of a knowledge commodity and the significance of critically assessing reified accounts of the origin of management ideas. This may support the need for students of management to recognize how different elements of management knowledge commodities may have their own evolution pattern and how elements of a management idea that moved through a period of stabilization and closure (Bijker, 1990) can become part of a new configuration of ideas and practices. These elements may become constantly reshaped, forgotten, and/or regarded as 'normal practice' which makes them less recognizable as part of the management idea they were initially associated with (see also Heusinkveld and Benders, 2012). Hence, studying the social life of management ideas in praxis remains a complex and difficult endeavor and that this work can be considered only a first step into this area.

Finally, this study has developed a critique on the assumed transient cycles in the supply of management solutions, or in the words of Gill and Whittle (1993) '. . . the cyclical and noncumulative nature of much of what passes for consulting approaches to organizational change and effectiveness' (1993: 292). However, at the same time, the research shows that it cannot be assumed that consultants or other knowledge entrepreneurs involved in the supply of management ideas will not reinvent the wheel. Lammers (1988) shows a strong ambivalence towards this phenomenon. While he acknowledged that popular management ideas may play an important role in repeatedly drawing attention to particular management knowledge, he also pointed out that these supply-side dynamics contribute to conditions under which management knowledge is likely to erode. An inability to systematically build on existing insights and experiences is not only at odds with the academic dictum of knowledge accumulation, but also entails that management practitioners have to reinvent what others already knew and therefore are condemned to endlessly repeat the same basic mistakes (Lammers, 1988; ten Bos, 2000; Benders and Vermeulen, 2002). Brunsson and Olsen (1997) even stress that the constant reintroduction of 'old' ideas benefits from and maintains organizational forgetfulness. Such collective forgetfulness ensures that earlier experiences do not obstruct the introductions of new commodities carrying similar problems now under a different label. Therefore developing sensitivity to issues around the social life of management ideas is not only a crucial issue for management scholars, but also has important implications for management praxis.

Appendix I
Consultant Informants

Appendix Table 1

Firm				Informant		
Code	Origin	Size*	Background	Code	Level	Background
A	International	Medium	Strategy	A1	Director	Business Administration
B	National	Medium	IT	B1	Senior consultant	Information Science
				B2	Managing consultant	Computer Science, PhD
				B3	Director	Computer Science
				B4	Senior consultant	Business Administration
				B5	Junior consultant	Information Science
				B6	Senior consultant	Information Science
C	National	Large	General mgt.	C1	Senior consultant	Business Engineering
				C2	Senior consultant	Mathematics
D	National	Small	IT	D1	Director	Electrical Engineering, PhD
E	National	Small	Strategy	E1	Senior consultant	Law, MBA
F	International	Large	IT	F1	Senior consultant	Economics
				F2	Managing consultant	Information Science
G	National	Small	Public mgt.	G1	Senior consultant	Business Administration
H	International	Large	IT	H1	Managing consultant	Physics
I	International	Medium	IT	I1	Senior consultant	Computer Science
				I2	Managing consultant	Information Science
J	National	Large	IT	J1	Managing consultant	Philosophy, PhD
K	International	Large	Accounting	K1	Managing consultant	Information Science
				K2	Junior consultant	Business Economics
				K3	Director	Psychology, MBA
				K4	Managing consultant	Medicine

L	International	Medium	General mgt.	L1	Director	Not available
				L2	Junior consultant	Law
M	National	Large	IT	M1	Junior consultant	Business Administration
				M2	Managing consultant	Chemistry
N	National	Medium	HRM	N1	Managing consultant	Psychology
				N2	Senior consultant	Water Engineering, PhD
O	National	Small	General mgt.	O1	Senior consultant	Chemistry, PhD
P	International	Large	Accounting	P1	Managing consultant	Mechanical Engineering
				P2	Senior consultant	Mechanical Engineering
				P3	Managing consultant	Business Economics
				P4	Director	Architecture, MBA
Q	National	Medium	Strategy	Q1	Director	Computer Science, PhD
				Q2	Senior consultant	Economics
R	International	Medium	General mgt.	R1	Senior consultant	Not available
S	National	Small	IT	S1	Managing consultant	Mechanical Engineering
T	International	Large	Accounting	T1	Managing consultant	Accounting
				T2	Managing consultant	Accounting
U	National	Medium	General mgt.	U1	Senior consultant	Business Administration
V	National	Small	General mgt.	V1	Junior consultant	Business Economics
				V2	Director	Psychology
				V3	Junior consultant	Health School
W	National	Large	General mgt.	W1	Managing consultant	Business Administration
				W2	Senior consultant	Business Administration
X	International	Large	Accounting	X1	Senior consultant	Chemistry

* Small < 50 employees, medium 50–250 employees, large > 250 employees.

Appendix II
Publications by Consultant Informants

Appendix Table 2

Code	Year	Genre	#Pages	Publication — *Main response strategy*
B1a	1998	Article	4	*Streamlining:* User orientation enhances BPR implementation
B2a	2000	Article	8	*Refocusing:* Deployment of formalized business process analysis approach to BPR rather than participatory approaches
B2b	2003	Article	4	*Normalizing:* BPR as common in Workflow Management (WFM) concept
B2c	2004	Article	4	*Relabeling:* Replace BPR with Business Process Management (BPM) concept
B4a	1998	Article	8	*Refocusing:* Deployment of formalized business process analysis approach to BPR rather than participatory approaches
B5a	2004	Article	4	*Normalizing:* BPR as common in Workflow Management (WFM) concept
C1a	2004	Article	2	*Relabeling:* Replace BPR with Business Process Management (BPM) concept
C2a	1998	Article	7	*Streamlining:* Suggestions to enhance the application of BPR
D1a	1999	Article	16	*Standardizing:* Advance systematization of BPR approach
D1b	2003	Article	5	*Streamlining:* Using architectures enhances success of BPR projects
D1c	2004	Article	4	*Relabeling:* Replace BPR with Business Process Management (BPM) concept
D1d	2003	Article	5	*Relabeling:* Replace BPR with E-business concept
F2a	1993	Article	4	*Refocusing:* Use of simulation in BPR rather than intuitive approach
I1a	1997	Article	11	*Normalizing:* Include BPR as common in Workflow Management (WFM)
I1b	2000	Article	7	*Relabeling:* Replace BPR by Business Process Management (BPM) concept
I1c	2001	Article	7	*Relabeling:* Replace BPR by Straight Through Processing (STP) concept
I1d	2001	Article	6	*Relabeling:* Replace BPR by Straight Through Processing (STP) concept
J1a	1999	Article	4	*Normalizing:* BPR as common practice in change trajectories
J1b	2000	Article	2	*Normalizing:* BPR as common in Data warehousing services

Code	Year	Type	No.	Description
K1a	1993	Article	4	*Refocusing*: Deployment of a multidisciplinary approach to BPR rather than mono-disciplinary
K1b	1993	Article	13	*Broadening*: BPR also useful for IT implementation and strategic positioning
K1c	1995	Book	158	*Standardizing*: Coherent BPR approach including methods and techniques
K1d	2001	Article	6	*Relabeling*: Replace BPR with Knowledge Management (KM) concept
K4a	1999	Book	164	*Relocating*: BPR as appropriate approach in the Health care sector
K4b	2000	Article	3	*Relocating*: BPR as appropriate approach in the Health care sector
N2a	1997	Article	8	*Refocusing*: Deployment of an HRM approach to BPR rather than technical
P4a	1994	Article	4	*Standardizing*: Codified lessons from BPR practice
P4b	1995	Article	5	*Streamlining*: More attention to change management enhances BPR success
P4c	1997	Article	5	*Broadening*: Apply BPR also to achieve growth, not only to cut costs
Q1a	1994	Article	4	*Broadening*: BPR also useful for enhancing value of IT investments
Q1b	2000	Article	11	*Normalizing*: BPR as useful approach in Balanced Scorecard projects
Q1c	2000	Article	9	*Relabeling*: Replace BPR with E-business
Q1d	2001	Article	9	*Relabeling*: Replace BPR with Outsourcing
Q2a	1992	Article	11	*Standardizing*: Emphasis on step approach to support BPR implementation
Q2b	1993	Article	6	*Streamlining*: Suggestions to improve BPR implementation success
Q2c	1994	Article	7	*Refocusing*: Focus on strategic approach to BPR rather than operational
Q2d	1997	Article	8	*Streamlining*: Cyclical approach to BPR to increase implementation success
Q2e	2000	Article	6	*Broadening*: BPR as useful approach in post-merger integration issues
Q2f	2002	Article	9	*Broadening*: BPR as useful approach in mergers of IT departments
Q2g	2003	Article	8	*Broadening*: BPR as useful approach in post-merger integration issues
T1a	1995	Article	5	*Standardizing*: Importance of codification of experiences with BPR projects
T1b	1996	Book	91	*Standardizing*: Coherent BPR approach including methods and techniques
T2a	1995	Article	5	*Standardizing*: Importance of codification of experiences with BPR projects

(*Continued*)

Appendix Table 2 (continued)

Code	Year	Genre	#Pages	Publication Main response strategy
U1a	1999	Article	7	*Refocusing*: Emphasis on translating BPR change into organizational structures
V2a	1993	Article	11	*Refocusing*: Emphasis on change management in BPR projects rather than IT implementation
V2b	1996	Article	4	*Broadening*: BPR also applied to designing new processes and efficacy issue rather than only efficiency
V2c	1997	Article	4	*Broadening*: BPR also applied to a range of new organizational problems
V3a	2001	Article	1	*Relocating*: BPR as a appropriate method in Health care organizations
W1a	1996	Book	116	*Relocating*: BPR as appropriate method in Banking and Insurance sectors

References

Abbott, A. (1988). *The system of professions*: *An essay on the division of expert labor*. Chicago: University of Chicago Press.

Abrahamson, E. (1996). Management fashion. *Academy of Management Review*, 21 (1), 254–85.

Abrahamson, E. (1997). The emergence and prevalence of employee management rhetorics: The effects of long waves, labor unions and turnover, 1875 to 1992. *Academy of Management Journal*, 40 (3), 491–533.

Abrahamson, E., and Eisenman, M. (2008). Employee-management techniques: Transient fads or trending fashions? *Administrative Science Quarterly*, 53 (4), 719–44.

Abrahamson, E., and Fairchild, G. (1999). Management fashion: Lifecycles, triggers and collective learning processes. *Administrative Science Quarterly*, 44 (4), 708–40.

Adair, S. (2010). The commodification of information and social inequality. *Critical Sociology*, 36 (2), 243–63.

Adams, M., Day, G., and Dougherty, D. (1998). Enhancing new product development performance: An organizational learning perspective. *Journal of Product Innovation Management*, 15 (3), 403–22.

Alvesson, M. (1993). Organizations as rhetoric: Knowledge-intensive firms and the struggle with ambiguity. *Journal of Management Studies*, 30 (6), 997–1015.

Alvesson, M. (2001). Knowledge work: Ambiguity, image and identity. *Human Relations*, 54 (7), 863–86.

Alvesson, M., Karreman, D., Sturdy, A., and Handley, K. (2009). Unpacking the client(s): Constructions, positions and client-consultant dynamics. *Scandinavian Journal of Management*, 25 (3), 253–63.

Anand, N., Gardner, H., and Morris, T. (2007). Knowledge-based innovation: Emergence and embedding of new practice areas in management consulting firms. *Academy of Management Journal*, 50 (2), 406–28.

Ansari, S., Fiss, P., & Zajac, E. (2010). Made to fit: How practices vary as they diffuse. *Academy of Management Review*, 35 (1), 67–92.

Appadurai, A. (1986). *The social life of things*: *Commodities in a cultural perspective*. Cambridge: Cambridge University Press.

Appadurai, A. (2005). Commodities and the politics of value. In M. Ertman and J. Williams (Eds.), *Rethinking commodification*: *Cases and readings in Law and Culture*, pp. 34–43. New York: New York University Press.

Argyris, C. (1961). Explorations in consulting-client relationships. *Human Organization*, 20 (3), 121–133.

Astley, W., and Zammuto, R. (1992). Organization science, managers and language games. *Organization Science*, 3 (4), 443–60.

Barley, S., and Kunda, G. (1992). Design and devotion: Surges of rational and normative ideologies of control in managerial discourse. *Administrative Science Quarterly*, 37 (3), 363–99.

Barley, S., Meyer, G., and Gash, D. (1988). Culture of cultures: Academics, practitioners and the pragmatics of normative control. *Administrative Science Quarterly*, 33 (2), 24–60.

Beck, N., and Walgenbach, P. (2005). Technical efficiency or adaptation to institutionalized expectations? The adoption of ISO 9000 standards in the German mechanical engineering industry. *Organization Studies*, 26 (6), 841–66.

Becker, H. (1974). Art as collective action. *American Sociological Review*, 39 (6), 767–76.

Benders, J. (1999). Tricks and trucks: A case study of organization concepts at work. *The International Journal of Human Resource Management*, 10 (4), 624–37.

Benders, J., Nijholt, J., and Heusinkveld, S. (2007). Using print media indicators in researching organization concepts. *Quality and Quantity*, 41 (6), 815–29.

Benders, J., and van Bijsterveld, M. (2000). Leaning on lean: The reception of a management fashion in Germany. *New Technology, Work and Employment*, 15 (1), 50–64.

Benders, J., van den Berg, R.J., and van Bijsterveld, M. (1998). Hitchhiking on a hype: Dutch consultants engineering re-engineering. *Journal of Organizational Change Management*, 11 (3), 201–15.

Benders, J., and van Veen, K. (2001). What's in a fashion? Interpretative viability and management fashion. *Organization*, 8 (1), 33–53.

Benders, J., and Verlaar, S. (2003). Lifting parts: Putting conceptual insights into practice. *International Journal of Operations and Production Management*, 23 (7), 757–74.

Benders, J., and Vermeulen, P. (2002). Too many tools? On problem solving in NPD projects. *International Journal of Innovation Management*, 6 (2), 163–185.

Bendix, R. (1956). *Work and authority in industry*. London: Wiley.

Benghozi, P.J. (1990). Managing innovation: From ad-hoc to routine in French telecom. *Organization Studies*, 11 (4), 531–54.

Berger, P., and Luckmann, T. (1966). *The social construction of reality*. New York: Doubleday.

Berglund, J., and Werr, A. (2000). The invincible character of management consulting rhetoric: How one blends incommensurates while keeping them apart. *Organization*, 7 (4), 633–55.

Bijker, W. (1990). *The social construction of technology*. Enschede: Alfa.

Birkinshaw, J., Hamel, G., and Mol, M. (2008). Management innovation. *Academy of Management Review*, 33 (4), 825–45.

Bloomfield, B., and Danieli, A. (1995). The role of management consultants in the development of information technology: The indissoluble nature of socio-political and technical skills. *Journal of Management Studies*, 32 (1), 23–46.

Bloomfield, B., and Vurdubakis, T. (1994). Re-presenting technology: IT consultancy reports as textual reality constructions. *Sociology*, 28 (2), 455–77.

Bocock, R. (1993). *Consumption*. New York: Routledge.

Boiral, O. (2003). ISO 9000: Outside the iron cage. *Organization Science*, 14 (6), 720–37.

Bourdieu, P. (1990). *The logic of practice*. Cambridge: Polity Press.

Boxenbaum, E., and Jonsson, S. (2008). Isomorphism, diffusion and decoupling. In R. Greenwood, C. Oliver, K. Sahlin, and R. Suddaby (Eds.), *The Sage handbook of organizational institutionalism*, pp. 78–98. Thousand Oaks, CA: Sage.

Braam, G., Benders, J., and Heusinkveld, S. (2007). The Balanced Scorecard in the Netherlands: An analysis of its evolution using print-media indicators. *Journal of Organizational Change Management*, 20 (6), 866–79.

Brown, A., and Ennew, C. (1995). Market research and the politics of new product development. *Journal of Marketing Management*, 11 (4), 339–54.

Brunsson, N. (1982). The functions of project evaluation. *R and D Management*, 10 (2), 147–60.

Brunsson, N. (1989). *The organization of hypocrisy: Talk, decisions and actions in organizations*. London: Routledge.

Brunsson, N., and Olsen, J. (1997). *The reforming organization*. Bergen/Sandviken: Fagbokforlaget.

Burgelman, R. (1983a). A process model of internal corporate venturing in the diversified major firm. *Administrative Science Quarterly*, 28 (2), 223–44.

Burgelman, R. (1983b). Corporate entrepreneurship and strategic management: Insights from a process study. *Management Science*, 29 (12), 1349–63.

Burns, T., and Stalker, G. (1961). *The management of innovation*. London: Tavistock.

Carson, P., Lanier, P., Carson, K., and Guidry, B. (1999). Clearing a path through the management fashion jungle: Some preliminary trailblazing. *Academy of Management Journal*, 43 (6), 1143–58.

Carter, C., and Crowther, D. (2000). Organizational consumerism: The appropriation of packaged managerial knowledge. *Management Decision*, 38 (9), 626–37.

Chakrabarti, A. (1974). The role of champion in product innovation. *California Management Review*, 17 (2), 58–62.

Clark, K.B., and Fujimoto, T. (1991). *Product development performance*. Boston, MA: Harvard Business School Press.

Clark, T. (1995). *Managing consultants: Consultancy as the management of impressions*. Buckingham, U.K.: Open University Press.

Clark, T. (2004). The fashion of management fashion: A surge too far? *Organization*, 11 (2), 297–306.

Clark, T., and Fincham, R. (2002). *Critical consulting: New perspectives on the management advice industry*. Oxford: Blackwell Publishers.

Clark, T., and Greatbatch, D. (2002). Collaborative relationships in the creation and fashioning of management ideas: Gurus, editors and managers. In M. Kipping and L. Engwall (Eds.), *Management consulting: Emergence and dynamics of a knowledge industry*, pp. 129–145. Oxford: Oxford University Press, 2002.

Clark, T., and Greatbatch, D. (2004). Management fashion as image spectacle: The production of best-selling management books. *Management Communication Quarterly*, 17 (3), 396–424.

Clark, T. and Salaman, G. (1998). Telling tales: Management gurus' narratives and the construction of managerial identity. *Journal of Management Studies*, 35 (2), 127–161.

Cohen, W., and Levinthal, D. (1990). Absorptive capacity: A new perspective on learning and innovation. *Administrative Science Quarterly*, 35 (1), 128–152.

Cole, R. (1999). *Managing Quality fads: How American business learned to play the Quality game*. New York: Oxford University Press.

Collins, D. (2003). The branding of management knowledge: Rethinking management fads. *Journal of Organizational Change Management*, 16 (2): 186–204.

Cooper, R. (1983). The new production process: An empirically based classification scheme. *R and D Management*, 13 (3), 1–13.

Cooper, R., and Kleinschmidt, E. (1986). An investigation into the new product process: Steps, deficiencies and impact. *Journal of Product Innovation Management*, 3 (1), 71–85.

Cornelissen, J. (2011). *Stretching, switching and blending frames: Sensemaking in and around organizations*. Amsterdam: VU University.

Cornelissen, J., and Clarke, J. (2010). Imagining and rationalizing opportunities: Inductive reasoning and the creation and justification of new ventures. *Academy of Management Review*, 35 (4), 539–57.

Cornelissen, J., Holt, R., and Zundel, M. (2011). The role of analogy and metaphor in the framing and legitimization of strategic change. *Organization Studies*, 32 (12), 1701–16.

Corrigan, P. (1997). *The sociology of consumption*. London: Sage.

Coupland, J., Robinson, J., and Coupland, N. (1994). Frame negotiation in doctor-elderly patient negotiations. *Discourse and Society*, 5 (1), 89–124.

Craig, D. (2005). *Rip-Off! The scandalous inside story of the management consulting money machine*. London: The Original Book Company.

Crainer, S. (1997). *The Tom Peters phenomenon: Corporate man to corporate skunk*. Oxford: Capstone.

Czarniawska, B., and Mazza, C. (2003). Consulting as a liminal space. *Human Relations*, 56 (3), 267–90.

Czarniawska, B., and Sevón, G. (1996). *Translating organizational change*. Berlin: Walter de Gruyter.

Daft, R., and Weick, K. (1984). Toward a model of organizations as interpretation systems. *Academy of Management Review*, 9 (2), 284–95.

Davis, M. (1986). 'That's classic!' The phenomenology and rhetoric of successful social theories. *Philosophy of Social Science*, 16 (3), 285–301.

D'Aunno, T., Succi, M., and Alexander, J. (2000). The role of institutional and market forces in divergent organizational change. *Administrative Science Quarterly*, 45 (4), 679–703.

David, R., and Strang, D. (2006). When fashion is fleeting: Transitory collective beliefs and the dynamics of TQM consulting. *Academy of Management Journal*, 49 (2), 215–33.

Day, G. (1994). The capabilities of market-driven organizations. *Journal of Marketing*, 58 (4), 37–52.

DeCock, C., and Hipkin, I. (1997). TQM and BPR: Beyond the beyond myth. *Journal of Management Studies*, 34 (5), 659–75.

Deephouse, D. (1999). To be different or to be the same? It's a question and theory of strategic balance. *Strategic Management Journal*, 20 (2), 147–166.

Delmas, M., and Toffel, M. (2008). Organizational responses to environmental demands: Opening the black box. *Strategic Management Journal*, 29 (8), 1027–55.

de Man, A.P. and de Caluwé, L. (2010). Hoe innoveren adviseurs? *Management & Organisatie*, 64 (2), 37–52.

Deshpande, R., and Zaltman, G. (1982). Factors affecting the use of market research information: A path analysis. *Journal of Marketing Research*, 19 (1), 14–31.

Dougherty, D. (1996). Organizing for innovation. In S. Clegg, C. Hardy, and W. Nord, (Eds.), *Handbook of organization studies*, pp. 424–39. London: Sage.

Dougherty, D., and Hardy, C. (1996). Sustained product innovations in large mature organizations: Overcoming innovation-to-organization problems. *Academy of Management Journal*, 39 (5), 1120–53.

Dougherty, D., and Heller, T. (1994). The illegitimacy of successful product innovation in established firms. *Organization Science*, 5 (2), 200–18.

DuGay, P. (1996). *Consumption and identity at work*. London: Sage.

Dutton, J., Ashford, S., O'Neill, R., and Lawrence, K. (2001). Moves that matter: Issue selling and organizational change. *Academy of Management Journal*, 44 (4), 716–36.

Eastman, W., and Bailey, J. (1998). Mediating the fact-value antinomy: Patterns in managerial and legal rhetoric, 1890–1990. *Organization Science*, 9 (2), 232–45.

Easton, G., and Jarrell, S. (2000). Patterns in the deployment of Total Quality Management: An analysis of 44 leading companies. In R. Cole and W. Scott (Eds.), *The Quality movement and organization theory*, pp. 89–130. Thousand Oaks, CA: Sage.

Ertman, M., and Williams, J. (2005). *Rethinking commodification: Cases and readings in Law and Culture*. New York: New York University Press.

Faust, M. (2002). Consultancies as actors in knowledge arenas: Evidence from Germany. In M. Kipping and L. Engwall (Eds.), *Management consulting*, pp. 146–163. Oxford: Oxford University Press.

Feldman, M., and Pentland, B. (2003). Reconceptualizing organizational routines as a source of flexibility and change. *Administrative Science Quarterly*, 48 (1), 94–118.

Fincham, R. (1995). Business process reengineering and the commodification of management knowledge. *Journal of Marketing Management*, 11 (7), 707–19.

Fincham, R. (1999). The consultant-client relationship: Critical perspectives on the management of organizational change. *Journal of Management Studies*, 36 (3), 335–51.

Fincham, R. (2012). The client in the client-consultant relationship. In T. Clark and M. Kipping (Eds.), *The Oxford handbook of management consulting*, pp. 411–26. Oxford: Oxford University Press.

Fincham, R., Clark, T., Handley, K., and Sturdy, A. (2008). Configuring expert knowledge: The consultant as a sector specialist. *Journal of Organizational Behavior*, 29 (8), 1.145–1.160.

Fincham, R., and Evans, M. (1999). The consultants' offensive: Reengineering–From fad to technique. *New Technology Work and Employment*, 14 (1), 32–44.

Fine, B. (2002). *The world of consumption: The material and cultural revisited*. London: Routledge.

Fiss, P., and Zajac, E. (2006). The symbolic management of strategic change: Sensegiving via framing and decoupling. *Academy of Management Journal*, 49 (6), 1173–93.

Fligstein, N. (1997). Social skills and institutional theory. *The American Behavioral Scientist*, 40 (4), 397–405.

Fosstenløkken, S., Løwendahl, B., and Revang, Ø. (2003). Knowledge development through client interaction: A comparative study. *Organization Studies*, 24 (6), 859–80.

Frenkel, M. (2005). The politics of translation: How state-level political relations affect the cross-national travel of management ideas. *Organization*, 12 (2), 275–301.

Furusten, S. (1999). *Popular management books: How they are made and what they mean for organisations*. London: Routledge.

Furusten, S. (2009). Management consultants as improvising agents of stability. *Scandinavian Journal of Management*, 25 (3), 264–74.

Garrone, P., and Colombo, M. (1999). Market-driven design of innovative services: The case of multimedia home banking. *Technovation*, 19 (9), 537–49.

Gilbert, J. (2008). Against the commodification of everything: Anti-consumerist cultural studies in the age of ecological crisis. *Cultural Studies*, 22 (5), 551–66.

Gill, J., and Whittle, S. (1993). Management by panacea: Accounting for transience. *Journal of Management Studies*, 30 (2), 281–95.

Giroux, H. (2006). It was such a handy term: Management fashions and pragmatic ambiguity. *Journal of Management Studies*, 43 (6), 1227–60.

Glaser, B., and Strauss, A. (1967). *The discovery of grounded theory*. Chicago: Aldine.

Glückler, J., and Armbrüster, T. (2003). Bridging uncertainty in management consulting: The mechanisms of trust and networked reputation. *Organization Studies*, 24 (2), 269–97.

Greatbatch, D., and Clark, T. (2005). *Management speak: Why we listen to what management gurus tell us*. London: Routledge.

Greenwood, R., Diaz, A., Li, S., and Lorente, J. (2010). The multiplicity of institutional logics and the heterogeneity of organizational responses. *Organization Science*, 21 (4), 521–39.

Greenwood, R., and Hinings, R. (1996). Understanding radical organizational change: Bringing together the old and the new institutionalism. *Academy of Management Review*, 21 (1), 1022–54.

Greiner, L., and Metzger, R. (1983). *Consulting to management*. Englewood Cliffs, NJ: Prentice-Hall.

Grint, K. (1994). Reengineering history: Social resonances and business process reengineering. *Organization*, 1 (1), 179–202.

Grint, K. (1997). *Fuzzy management: Contemporary ideas and practices at work*. London: Blackwell.

Grint, K., and Case, P. (1998). The violent rhetoric of re-engineering: Management consultancy on the offensive. *Journal of Management Studies*, 35 (5), 557–77.

Guillén, M. (1994). *Models of management: Work, authority and organization in a comparative perspective*. Chicago: University of Chicago Press.

Hackman, J., and Wageman, R. (1995). TQM: Empirical, conceptual, and practical issues. *Administrative Science Quarterly*, 40 (2), 309–42.

Hammer, M., and Champy, J. (1993). *Reengineering the corporation: A manifesto for business revolution*. London: Nicolas Brealey.

Hansen, M.T., Nohria, N., and Tienery, T. (1999). What's your strategy for managing knowledge? *Harvard Business Review*, 77 (2), 106–116.

Hargadon, A., and Douglas, Y. (2001). When innovations meet institutions: Edison and the design of the electric light. *Administrative Science Quarterly*, 46 (3), 476–501.

Hellström, T., and Raman, S. (2001). The commodification of knowledge about knowledge: Knowledge management and reification of epistemology. *Social Epistemology*, 15 (3), 139–154.

Heusinkveld, S., and Benders, J. (2001). Surges and sediments: Shaping the reception of Reengineering. *Information and Management*, 38 (4), 239–51.

Heusinkveld, S., and Benders, J. (2002). Between professional dedication and corporate design: Exploring forms of new concept development in consultancies. *International Studies of Management and Organization*, 32 (4), 104–122.

Heusinkveld, S., and Benders, J. (2005). Contested commodification: Consultancies and their struggle with new concept development. *Human Relations*, 58 (3), 283–310.

Heusinkveld, S., and Benders, J. (2012a). On sedimentation in management fashion: An institutional perspective. *Journal of Organizational Change Management*, 25 (1), 121–142.

Heusinkveld, S., and Benders, J. (2012b). Consultants and organization concepts. In T. Clark & M. Kipping (Eds.), *The Oxford handbook of management consulting*, pp. 267–84. Oxford: Oxford University Press.

Heusinkveld, S., Benders, J., and Hillebrand, B. (2013). Stretching concepts: The role of competing pressures and decoupling in the evolution of organization concepts. *Organization Studies*, 34 (1), 7–32.

Heusinkveld, S., Benders, J., and van den Berg, R.J. (2009). From market sensing to new concept development in consultancies: The role of information processing and organizational capabilities. *Technovation*, 29 (8), 506–518.

Heusinkveld, S., and Reijers, H. (2009). Reflections on a reflective cycle: Building legitimacy in design knowledge development. *Organization Studies*, 30 (8), 865–886.

Heusinkveld, S., Sturdy, A. and Werr, A. (2011). The co-consumption of management ideas and practices. *Management Learning*, 42 (2), 139–147.

Heusinkveld, S., and Visscher, K. (2012). Practice what you preach: How consultants frame management concepts as enacted practice. *Scandinavian Journal of Management*, 28 (4), 285–297.

Hilmer, F., and Donaldson, L. (1996). *Management redeemed: Rebunking the fads that undermine our corporations*. New York: The Free Press.

Hirsch, P. (1972). Processing fads and fashions: An organization-set analysis of cultural industry systems. *American Journal of Sociology*, 77 (4), 639–59.

Hirsch, P., and Bermiss, S. (2009). Institutional 'dirty' work: Preserving institutions through strategic decoupling. In T. Lawrence, R. Suddaby, and B. Leca (Eds.), *Institutional work: Actors and agency in institutional studies of organizations*, pp. 262–83. Cambridge: Cambridge University Press.

Hislop, D. (2002). The client role in consultancy relations during the appropriation of technological innovations. *Research Policy*, 31 (5), 657–71.

Holtz, H. (1983). *How to succeed as an independent consultant*. New York: Wiley.

Howard-Grenville, J. (2005). The persistence of flexible organizational routines: The role of agency and organizational context. *Organization Science*, 16 (6), 618–36.

Huczynski, A. (1993). *Management gurus: What makes them and how to become one*. London: Routledge.

Jackson, B. (1996). Re-engineering the sense of self: The manager and the management guru. *Journal of Management Studies*, 33 (5), 571–90.

Jackson, B. (2001). *Management gurus and management fashions: A dramatistic inquiry*. London: Routledge.

Jacques, R. (1996). *Manufacturing the employee: Management knowledge from the 19th to 21st centuries*. London: Sage.

Jarzabkowski, P. (2004). Strategy as practice: Recursiveness, adaptation, and practice-in-use. *Organization Studies*, 25 (4), 529–60.

Jarzabkowski, P., Balogun, J., and Seidl, D. (2007). Strategizing: The challenges of a practice perspective. *Human Relations*, 60 (1), 5–27.

Jelinck, M., and Schoonhoven, C.B. (1990). *The innovation marathon: Lessons from high technology firms*. Oxford: Basil Blackwell.

Jones, M., and Thwaites, R. (2000). Dedicated followers of fashion: BPR and the public sector. In D. Knights and H. Willmott (Eds.), *The Reengineering revolution; Critical studies of corporate change*, pp. 50–62. London: Sage.

Jones, O., and Stevens, G. (1999). Evaluating failure in the innovation process: The micropolitics of new product development. *R&D Management*, 29 (2), 167–178.

Kelemen, M. (2000). Too much or too little ambiguity: The language of Total Quality Management. *Journal of Management Studies*, 37 (4), 483–98.

Kieser, A. (1996). Business Process Reengineering—Neue Kleider für den Kaiser? *Zeitschrift Führung und Organisation*, 65 (3), 179–185.

Kieser, A. (1997). Rhetoric and myth in management fashion. *Organization*, 4 (1), 49–74.

Kieser, A. (2002). Managers as marionettes? Using fashion theories to explain the success of consultancies. In M. Kipping and L. Engwall (Eds.), *Management consulting: Emergence and dynamics of a knowledge industry*, pp. 167–183. Oxford: Oxford University Press.

Kieser, A. (2002). On communication barriers between management science, consultancies and business organizations. In T. Clark and R. Fincham (Eds.), *Critical consulting: New perspectives on the management advice industry*, pp. 206–27. Oxford: Blackwell.

Kipping, M. (1999). American management consulting companies in Western Europe, 1920s to 1990s: Products, reputation and relationships. *Business History Review*, 73 (2), 190–220.

Kipping, M. (2002). Trapped in their wave: The evolution of management consultancies. In T. Clark and R. Fincham (Eds.), *Critical consulting: New perspectives on the management advice industry*, pp. 18–49. Oxford: Blackwell Publishers.

Kipping, M., and Clark, T. (2012). *The Oxford handbook of management consulting*. Oxford: Oxford University Press.

Kipping, M., and Engwall, L. (2002). *Management consulting: Emergence and dynamics of a knowledge industry*. Oxford: Oxford University Press.

Kitay, J., and Wright, C. (2004). Take the money and run? Organisational boundaries and consultants' roles. *The Service Industries Journal*, 24 (3), 1–18.

Knights, D., and McCabe, D. (1998). What happens when the phone goes wild? Staff, stress and spaces for escape in a BPR telephone banking work regime. *Journal of Management Studies*, 35 (2), 163–194.

Kohli, A., and Jaworski, B. (1990). Market orientation: The construct, research propositions, and managerial implications. *Journal of Marketing*, 54 (2), 1–18.

Kok, R., Hillebrand, B., and Biemans, W. (2003). What makes product development market oriented? Towards a conceptual framework. *International Journal of Innovation Management*, 7 (2), 137–162.

Kopytoff, I. (1982). Slavery. *Annual Review of Anthropology*, 11 (1), 207–30.

Kopytoff, I. (1986). The cultural biography of things: Commoditization as process. In A. Appadurai (Ed.), *The social life of things: Commodities in cultural perspective*, pp. 64–91. Cambridge: Cambridge University Press.

Kraatz, M., and Zajac, E. (1996). Exploring the limits of the new institutionalism: The causes and consequences of illegitimate organizational change. *American Sociological Review*, 61 (5), 812–36.

Kumar, R., and Das, T.K. (2007). Interpartner legitimacy in the alliance development process. *Journal of Management Studies*, 44 (8), 1425–53.

Lammers, C. (1986). De excellente onderneming als organisatiemodel. *Harvard Holland Review*, 3 (8), 18–27.

Lammers, C. (1988). Transience and persistence of ideal types in organization theory. In N. DiTomaso and S. Bacharach (Eds.), *Research in the sociology of organizations*, pp. 203–24. Greenwich, CT: JAI Press.

Lawrence, P., and Lorsch, J. (1967). *Organization and environment: Managing differentiation and integration*. Boston, MA: Division of Research, Graduate School of Business Administration, Harvard University.

Lewis, M.W., Welsh, M.A., Dehler, G.E., and Green, S.G. (2002). Product development tensions: Exploring contrasting styles of project management. *Academy of Management Journal*, 45 (3), 546–64.

Loader, I. (1999). Consumer culture and the commodification of policing and security. *Sociology*, 33 (2), 373–92.

Løwendahl, B., and Revang, O. (2004). Achieving results in an after modern context. *European Management Review*, 1 (1), 49–54.

Lyotard, J.F. (1984). *The postmodern condition*. Manchester: Manchester University Press.

March, J. (1981). Footnotes to organizational change. *Administrative Science Quarterly*, 26 (4), 563–77.

Marchington, M., Wilkinson, A., Ackers, P., and Goodman, J. (1993). The influence of managerial relations on waves of employee involvement. *British Journal of Industrial Relations*, 31 (4), 553–76.

McGill, M. (1988). *American business and the quick fix*. New York: Henry Holt.

McKenna, C. (1997). The American challenge: McKinsey & Company's role in the transfer of decentralization to Europe, 1957–1975. *Academy of Management Best Papers Proceedings*, pp. 226–230. San Francisco: Academy of Management.

McKenna, C. (2006). *The world's newest profession: Management consulting in the twentieth century*. New York: Cambridge University Press.

Meyer, J., and Rowan, B. (1977). Institutionalized organizations: Formal structure as myth and ceremony. *American Journal of Sociology*, 83 (2), 340–63.

Micklethwait, J., and Wooldridge, A. (1996). *The witch doctors: What the management gurus are saying, why it matters and how to make sense of it*. London: Heinemann.

Miettinen, R., Samra-Fredericks, D., and Yanow, D. (2009). Re-turn to practice: An introductory essay. *Organization Studies*, 30 (12), 1309–27.

Miles, M., and Huberman, M. (1994). *Qualitative data analysis*. Thousand Oaks, CA: Sage.

Miller, C., Cardinal, L., and Glick, W. (1997). Retrospective reports in organizational research: A reexamination of recent evidence. *Academy of Management Journal*, 40 (1), 189–204.

Mohe, M., and Seidl, D. (2011). Theorizing the client-consultant relationship from the perspective of social-systems theory. *Organization*, 18 (1), 3–22.

Moorman, C., and Miner, A.S. (1998). The convergence of planning and execution: Improvisation in new product development. *Journal of Marketing*, 62 (3), 1–20.

Morris, T. (2001). Asserting property rights: Knowledge codification in the professional service firm. *Human Relations*, 54 (7), 819–38.

Morris, T., and Empson, L. (1998). Organization and expertise: An exploration of knowledge bases and the management of accounting and consulting firms. *Accounting, Organization and Society*, 23 (5/6), 609–624.

Mueller, F., and Whittle, A. (2011). Translating management ideas: A discursive device analysis. *Organization Studies*, 32 (2), 187–210.

Nelson, D. (1975). *Managers and workers: Origins of the new factory system in the United States, 1880–1920*. Madison: University of Wisconsin Press.

Nicolai, A., and Dautwiz, J. (2010). Fuzziness in action: What consequences has the linguistic ambiguity of the core competence concept for organizational usage? *British Journal of Management*, 21 (4), 874–88.

Nicolai, A., and Thomas, T. (2006). De-diversification activities of German corporations from 1988 to 2002: Perspectives from agency and management fashion theory. *Schmalenbach Business Review*, 58 (1), 56–80.

Nijholt, J., and Benders, J. (2007). Co-evolution in management fashions: The case of self-managed teams in the Netherlands. *Group and Organization Management*, 32 (6), 628–52.

Nijholt, J., and Benders, J. (2010). Measuring the prevalence of self-managing teams. *Work, Employment and Society*, 24 (2), 375–385.

Nikolova, N., Reihlen, M., and Schlappfen, J.F. (2009). Client-consultant interaction: Capturing social practices of professional service production. *Scandinavian Journal of Management*, 25 (3), 289–98.

O'Mahoney, J. (2007). The diffusion of management innovations: The possibilities and limitations of memetics. *Journal of Management Studies*, 44 (8), 1324–48.

O'Mahoney, J. (2010). *Management consultancy*. New York: Oxford University Press.

O'Mahoney, J. (2011). *Management innovation in the UK consulting industry*. London: Chartered Management Institute.

O'Mahoney, J., Heusinkveld, S., and Wright, C. (2013). Commodifying the commodifiers: The impact of procurement on management knowledge. *Journal of Management Studies*, 50 (2), 204–35.

O'Shea, J., and Madigan, C. (1997). *Dangerous company: The consulting powerhouses and the businesses they save and ruin*. London: Nicholas Brealey.

Oliver, C. (1991). Strategic responses to institutional pressures. *Academy of Management Review*, 16 (1), 145–179.

Oliver, C. (1992). The antecedents of deinstitutionalization. *Organization Studies*, 13 (4), 563–88.

Orihata, M., and Watanabe, C. (2000). Evolutionary dynamics of product innovation: The case of consumer electronics. *Technovation*, 20 (8), 437–49.

Orlikowski, W. (2002). Knowing in practice: Enacting a collective capacity in distributed organizing. *Organization Science*, 13 (3), 249–73.

Ortmann, G. (1995). *Formen der Produktion: Organisation und Rekursivität*. Opladen, Germany: Westdeutscher Verlag.

Pache, A., and Santos, F. (2010). When worlds collide: The internal dynamics of organizational responses to conflicting institutional demands. *Academy of Management Review*, 35 (3), 455–76.

Parker, M. (2002). *Against management: Organization in the age of managerialism*. Oxford: Polity.

Pascale, R. (1990). *Managing on the edge: How successful companies use conflict to stay ahead*. London: Penguin Books.

Pellegrini, S. (2002). Managing the interplay and tensions of consulting interventions: The consultant-client relationship as mediation and reconciliation. *Journal of Management Development*, 21 (5), 343–65.

Perkmann, M., and Spicer, A. (2008). How are management fashions institutionalized? The role of institutional work. *Human Relations*, 61 (6), 811–44.

Peters, P., and Heusinkveld, S. (2010). Institutional explanations for managers' attitudes towards Telehomeworking. *Human Relations*, 63 (1), 107–135.

Peterson, R.A. (1979). Revitalizing the culture concept. *Annual Review of Sociology*, 5 (1), 137–166.

Peterson, R.A., and Anand, N. (2004). The production of culture perspective. *Annual Review of Sociology*, 30 (1), 137–166.

Pettigrew, A. (1975). Towards a political theory of organizational intervention. *Human Relations*, 28 (3), 191–208.

Pinault, L. (2000). *Consulting demons: Inside the unscrupulous world of global corporate consulting*. Chichester, U.K.: Wiley.

Prasad, L., and Rubenstein, A. (1994). Power and organizational politics during new product development: A conceptual framework. *Journal of Scientific and Industrial Research*, 53 (6), 397–407.

Radder, H. (2010). *The commodification of academic research: Science and the modern university*. Pittsburgh: University of Pittsburgh Press.

Radin, M. (2001). *Contested commodities*. Cambridge, MA: Harvard University Press.

Reihlen, M., and Nikolova, N. (2010). Knowledge production in consulting teams. *Scandinavian Journal of Management*, 26 (3), 279–89.

Reijers, H.A. (2003). *Design and control of workflow processes: Business process management for the service industry*. Berlin: Springer-Verlag.

Rogers, E.M. (1995). *Diffusion of innovations*. New York: Free Press.

Røvik, K.A. (1996). Deinstitutionalization and the logic of fashion. In B. Czarniawska and G. Sevón (Eds.), *Translating organizational change*, pp. 139–172. Berlin: Walter de Gruyter.

Røvik, K.A. (2002). The secrets of the winners: Management ideas that flow. In K. Sahlin-Andersson and L. Engwall (Eds.), *The expansion of management knowledge: Carriers, ideas and sources*, pp. 113–144. Stanford: Stanford University Press.

Røvik, K.A. (2011). From fashion to virus: An alternative theory of organizations' handling of management ideas. *Organization Studies*, 32 (5), 631–53.

Sahlin-Andersson, K., and Engwall, L. (2002). *The expansion of management knowledge: Carriers, flows and sources*. Stanford: Stanford University Press.

Sarvary, M. (1999). Knowledge management and competition in the consulting industry. *California Management Review*, 41 (2), 95–107.

Scarbrough, H., and Swan J. (2001). Explaining the diffusion of knowledge management: The role of fashion. *British Journal of Management*, 12 (1), 3–12.

Schön, D. (1983). *The reflective practitioner*. New York: Basic Books.

Schoonoven, C.B., and Jelinek, M. (1997). Dynamic tension in innovative, high technological firms: Managing rapid technological change through organizational structure. In M.L. Tushman and P. Anderson (Eds.), *Managing strategic innovation and change: A collection of readings*, pp. 233–54. New York: Oxford University Press.

Scott, R. (2001). *Institutions and organizations*. Thousand Oaks, CA: Sage.

Sharma, A. (1997). Professional as agent: Knowledge asymmetry in agency exchange. *Academy of Management Review*, 22 (3), 758–98.

Shenhav, Y. (1999). *Manufacturing rationality: The engineering foundations of the managerial revolution*. Oxford: Oxford University Press.

Sinha, V. (2011). *Religion and commodification: Merchandizing diasporic Hinduism*. New York: Routledge.

Sorge, A., and van Witteloostuijn, A. (2004). The (non)sense of organizational change: An essai about universal management hypes, sick consultancy metaphors, and healthy organization theories. *Organization Studies*, 25 (8), 1205–31.

Spell, C. (2001). Management fashions: Where do they come from, and are they old wine in new bottles? *Journal of Management Inquiry*, 10 (4), 358–73.

Staw, B., and Epstein, L. (2000). What bandwagons may bring: Effects of popular management techniques on corporate performance, reputation and CEO pay. *Administrative Science Quarterly*, 45 (3), 523–56.

Stinchcombe, A. (1965). Social structure and organizations. In J. March (Ed.), *Handbook of organizations*, pp. 142–193. Chicago: Rand McNally.

Stjernberg, T., and Philips, Å. (1993). Organizational innovations in a long-term perspective: Legitimacy and souls of fire as critical factors of change and viability. *Human Relations*, 46 (10), 1193–1220.

Strang, D. (2010). *Learning by example: Imitation and innovation at a global bank*. Princeton: Princeton University Press.

Strang, D., and Meyer, J. (1993). Institutional conditions for diffusion. *Theory and Society*, 22 (4), 487–511.

Strauss, A., and Corbin, J. (1998). *Basics of qualitative research: Techniques and procedures for developing grounded theory*. Thousand Oaks, CA: Sage.

Sturdy, A. (1997). The consultancy process–An insecure business? *Journal of Management Studies*, 34 (3), 389–413.

Sturdy, A. (2004). The adoption of management ideas and practices: Theoretical perspectives and possibilities. *Management Learning*, 35 (2), 155–179.

Sturdy, A. (2011). Consultancy's consequences: A critical assessment of management consultancy's impact on management. *British Journal of Management*, 22 (3), 517–30.

Sturdy, A., Brocklehurst, M., Winstanley, D., and Littlejohns, M. (2006). Management as a (self)confidence trick: Management ideas, education and identity work. *Organization*, 13 (6), 841–60.

Sturdy, A., Clark, T., Fincham, R., and Handley, K. (2009). *Management consultancy: Boundaries and knowledge in action*. Oxford: Oxford University Press.

Sturdy, A., and Gabriel, Y. (2000). Missionaries, mercenaries or car salesmen? MBA teaching in Malaysia. *Journal of Management Studies*, 37(7), 979–1002.

Sturdy, A., Werr, A., and Buono, A. (2009). The client in management consulting research: Mapping the territory. *Scandinavian Journal of Management*, 25 (3), 247–52.

Suchman, M. (1995). Managing legitimacy: Strategic and institutional approaches. *Academy of Management Review*, 20 (3), 571–610.

Suddaby, R., and Greenwood, R. (2001). Colonizing knowledge: Commodification as a dynamic of jurisdictional expansion in professional service firms. *Human Relations*, 54 (7), 933–53.

Szulanski, G. (1996). Exploring internal stickiness: Impediments to the transfer of best practices within the firm. *Strategic Management Journal*, 17 (4), 27–43.

Taminiau, Y., Smit, W., and de Lange, A. (2009). Innovation in management consulting firms through informal knowledge sharing. *Journal of Knowledge Management*, 13 (1), 42–55.

ten Bos, R. (2000). *Fashion and Utopia in management thinking*. Philadelphia: Benjamins.

ten Bos, R., and Heusinkveld, S. (2007). The gurus' gusto: Management fashion, performance and taste. *Journal of Organizational Change Management*, 20 (3), 304–25.

Tidd, J., Bessant, J., and Pavitt, K. (1997). *Managing innovation: Integrating technological, market and organizational change*. Chichester, U.K.: Wiley.

Tolbert, P., and Zucker, L. (1983). Institutional sources of change in the formal structure of organizations: The diffusion of civil service reform. *Administrative Science Quarterly*, 28 (1), 22–39.

Tolbert, P., and Zucker, L. (1996). Institutional theory. In C. Hardy, P. Frost, and S. Clegg (Eds.), *The Sage handbook of organization studies*, pp. 424–39. London: Sage.

Tsoukas, H. (1996). The firm as a distributed knowledge system: A constructionist approach. *Strategic Management Journal*, 17 (4), 11–25.

Twiss, B. (1992). *Managing technological innovation*. London: Longman.

van de Ven, A. (1986). Central problems in the management of innovation. *Management Science*, 32 (5), 590–607.

van de Ven, A. (1992). Suggestions for studying strategy process: A research note. *Strategic Management Journal*, 13 (S1), 169–188.

van Veen, K., Bezemer, J., and Karsten, L. (2011). Diffusion, translation and the neglected role of managers in the fashion setting process: The case of MANS. *Management Learning*, 42 (2), 149–164.

Vermeulen, P. (2001). *Organizing product innovation in financial services: How banks and insurance companies organize their innovation processes*. Nijmegen: Nijmegen University Press.

Vermeulen, P. (2005). Uncovering barriers to complex incremental product innovation in small and medium-sized financial services firms. *Journal of Small Business Management*, 43 (4), 432–52.

Visscher, K. (2001). *Design methodology in management consulting*. Enschede: University of Twente.

Visscher, K. (2006). Capturing the competence of management consulting work. *Journal of Workplace Learning*, 18 (4), 248–60.

Visscher, K., and Fisscher, O. (2009). Cycles and diamonds: How management consultants diverge and converge in organization design processes. *Creativity and Innovation Management*, 18 (2), 121–131.

Visscher, K., and Visscher-Voerman, J. (2010). Organizational design approaches in management consulting. *Management Decision*, 48 (5), 713–31.

Watson, T. (1986). *Management, organisation and employment strategy*. London: Routledge.

Watson, T. (1994). Management flavours of the month: Their role in managers' lives. *International Journal of Human Resource Management*, 5 (4), 892–909.

Werr, A. (1999). *The language of change: The roles of methods in the work of management consultants*. Stockholm: Stockholm School of Economics.

Werr, A. (2002). The internal creation of consulting knowledge: a question of structuring experience. In M. Kipping and L. Engwall (Eds.), *Management consulting: Emergence and dynamics of a knowledge industry*, pp. 91–108. Oxford: Oxford University Press.

Werr, A., and Stjernberg, T. (2003). Exploring management consulting firms as knowledge systems. *Organization Studies*, 24 (6), 881–908.

Werr, A., Stjernberg, T., and Docherty, P. (1997). The functions of methods of change in management consulting. *Journal of Organizational Change Management*, 10 (4), 288–307.

Wester, F. (1995). *Strategieën voor kwalitatief onderzoek* (Strategies for qualitative research). Bussum: Coutinho.

Westphal, J., and Zajac, E. (2001). Decoupling policy from practice: The case of stock repurchase programs. *Administrative Science Quarterly*, 46 (2), 202–28.

Wheelwright, S., and Clark, K. (1992). *Revolutionizing product development*. New York: Free Press.

Whittington, R. (2006). Completing the practice turn in strategy research. *Organization Studies*, 27 (5), 613–34.

Whittle, A. (2005). Preaching and practising 'flexibility': Implications for theories of subjectivity at work. *Human Relations*, 58 (10): 1301–22.

Whittle, A. (2006). The paradoxical repertoires of management consultancy. *Journal of Organizational Change Management*, 19 (4), 424–36.

Whittle, A. (2008). From flexibility to work-life balance: Exploring the changing discourses of management consultants. *Organization*, 15 (4), 513–34.

Wilhelm, H., and Bort, S. (2013). How managers talk about their consumption of popular management concepts: Identity, rules and situations. *British Journal of Management*, forthcoming.

Williams, J., and Zelizer, V. (2005). To commodify or not to Commodify: That is not the question. In M. Ertman and J. Williams (Eds.), *Rethinking commodification: Cases and readings in Law and Culture*, pp. 362–382. New York: New York University Press.

Willmott, H. (1995). Managing the academics: Commodification and control in the development of university education in the UK. *Human Relations*, 48 (9), 993–1027.

Woodward, J. (1965). *Industrial organization: Theory and practice*. London: Oxford University Press.

Wright, C. (2002). Promoting demand, gaining legitimacy and broadening expertise: the evolution of consultancy-client relationships in Australia. In M. Kipping and L. Engwall (Eds.), *Management consulting: Emergence and dynamics of a knowledge industry*, pp. 184–202. Oxford: Oxford University Press.

Wright, C., and Kitay, J. (2004). Spreading the word: Gurus, consultants and the diffusion of the Employee Relations paradigm in Australia. *Management Learning*, 35 (3), 271–86.

Yin, R. (1994). *Case study research: Design and methods*. Thousand Oaks, CA: Sage.

Zbaracki, M. (1998). The rhetoric and reality of total quality management. *Administrative Science Quarterly*, 43 (3), 602–36.

Zeitz, G., Mittal, V., and McAulay, B. (1999). Distinguishing adoption and entrenchment of management practices: A framework for analysis. *Organization Studies*, 20 (5), 741–76.

Index